Contents

Ellen Kottler • Jeffrey A. Kottler

Children With Limited English

Teaching Strategies for the Regular Classroom

Second Edition

CORWIN PRESS, INC.
A Sage Publications Company
Thousand Oaks, California

For information:

Corwin Press, Inc.
A Sage Publications Company
2455 Teller Road
Thousand Oaks, California 91320
E-mail: order@corwinpress.com

Sage Publications Ltd.
6 Bonhill Street
London EC2A 4PU
United Kingdom

Sage Publications India Pvt. Ltd.
M-32 Market
Greater Kailash I
New Delhi 110 048 India

Printed in the United States of America

Library of Congress Cataloging-in-Publication Data

Kottler, Ellen.
    Children with limited English: Teaching strategies for the regular classroom / by Ellen Kottler and Jeffrey A. Kottler.— 2nd ed.
        p. cm.
    Includes bibliographical references and index.
    ISBN 0-7619-7837-2 (cloth) — ISBN 0-7619-7838-0 (pbk.)
        1. English language—Study and teaching—Foreign speakers.
    2. Children of immigrants—Education—Language arts. 3. Language and education.   I. Kottler, Jeffrey A. II. Title.
    PE1128.A2 K68 2001
    428.0071—dc21   2001002905

This book is printed on acid-free paper.

04   05   06   07   7   6   5   4   3

Acquiring Editor:	Rachel Livsey
Corwin Editorial Assistant:	Phyllis Cappello
Production Editor:	Olivia Weber
Editorial Assistant:	Ester Marcelino
Typesetter/Designer:	Larry K. Bramble
Cover Designer:	Michael Dubowe
Copy Editor:	Rachel Hile Bassett
Indexer:	Janet Perlman

Preface

I f there is one challenge that teachers are likely to face in coming years, it will be working with an increasingly diverse student population. This will be true not only in terms of the cultural background of children, but also in terms of the languages they speak. Already in many schools around the continent, English is the native language for only a small minority of the school population. During recess periods, an astute observer can hear literally dozens of different languages being spoken in a single school. Needless to say, it makes for some *very* interesting work in the classroom when a significant number of students may not be able to communicate effectively with one another, much less understand the dominant language of instruction.

Whether students are recent immigrants, inhabitants of bilingual homes, or inhabitants of homes in which only native languages are spoken, they struggle tremendously with the burdens of not only keeping up with their schoolwork and establishing a social network, but also doing so with limited or nonexistent English-speaking skills. Their school performance suffers significantly; just as tragically, they may come to see themselves as worthless, stupid, or poor learners.

When such a child is first presented in the classroom doorway, many questions come to the teacher's mind: How can I possibly help this student when we don't even speak the same language? How will the other children react to having this child in their midst? How can I meet this child's special needs and provide a successful school experience? What can I do to make the adjustment easiest for all of us? And how can I do all this without exhausting myself in the process?

This ever more frequent situation does indeed present some obstacles. Fortunately, there are a number of options available to the regular classroom teacher who is looking for supplemental skills, ideas, and resources to better serve students acquiring English. The purpose of this book is to help teachers function more effectively with this student population and do so in such a way as to enhance rather than complicate their classroom environment.

Who Can Use This Book

This book is directed first to the population of beginning teachers who are being initiated into the realities of teaching as a career. It is overwhelming enough to think about managing a relatively homogeneous group of kids without contemplating the added complexities of working with a class in which the children don't all speak the same language. Useful strategies for limited-English students will thus augment a new teacher's repertoire. Indeed, some school districts organize support groups for new teachers in which they can talk about the issues and situations that confront them, such as working with limited-English students in the regular classroom. The survival skills presented here will serve as a handy reference for new teachers facing an increasingly diverse school population.

Next, students in teacher education courses will find this a good primary or supplementary text. As future teachers and student teachers prepare to meet the needs of diverse public school populations, this book addresses the concerns and fears of those who have not had the training or opportunity to work with students who are learning English as a second language.

Finally, veteran teachers who are experiencing professional transitions in their work, who may have logged years of experience in the classroom but who have had few opportunities to work with students new to the English language, will also find many of the concepts and methods described in this book quite useful.

Content and Process

The second edition of this book is twice as long as its predecessor. When this book was first published in 1994, it was one of the few resources available for practicing teachers. Since that time, there has been new research and many new teaching innovations that have been incorporated into contemporary practice. New to this edition are sections on cultural background, values, learning styles, multiple intelligences, and applications of brain research to the practice of teaching diverse students.

The progression of chapters follows a pattern that resembles quite closely what practicing teachers actually do when they face the challenge of helping non-English-speaking children. The first two chapters address the crucial task of developing a relationship with students in such a way as to build trust and establish a comfortable environment. Chapter 3 reviews principles related to second-language development, with attention to setting reasonable expectations in the classroom. Chapters 4, 5, and 6 present a number of practical teaching strategies, some of which make use of innovative structures and technology. Chapter 7 encourages teachers to expand the classroom by collaborating with other professionals in the school and in the community as a way to involve others in the learning process. Finally, Chapter 8 helps pull everything together.

It is quite clear that the future of our educational system in this country will be determined largely by our willingness and ability to help an increasingly diverse population of children who want their chance to reach their dreams.

Acknowledgments

We would like to thank President Gracia Alkema, copy editor Rachel Hile Bassett, the entire production staff of Corwin Press, and the following reviewers:

Carolyn M. Bowden
Associate Professor of Education
Salisbury State University
Salisbury, Maryland

Francesina R. Jackson
Assistant Dean
School of Education
North Carolina Central University
Durham, North Carolina

Sharon Toomey Clark
Massachusetts College of Liberal Arts
North Adams, Massachusetts

Elise J. Geither
Instructor, The American Language Academy
Baldwin-Wallace College
Berea, Ohio

Tery J. Medina
National Origin Coordinator
Southeastern Equity Center
Miami, Florida

Victoria Perruc
Lead Trainer, "Strategies for Teaching Content to English
    Language Learners"
Summer Staff Development
Gwinnett County Public Schools
Lawrenceville, Georgia

Susan Burke
High School and Social Studies Trainer, "Strategies for Teaching
    Content to English Language Learners"
Summer Staff Development
Gwinnett County Public Schools
Lawrenceville, Georgia

Ernie Blankenship
Middle, High School, and Science Trainer, "Strategies for
    Teaching Content to English Language Learners"
Summer Staff Development
Gwinnett County Public Schools/Richards Middle School
Lawrenceville, Georgia

Saundra Deltac
Elementary School Trainer, "Strategies for Teaching Content to
    English Language Learners"
Summer Staff Development
Hopkins Elementary School/Gwinnett County Public Schools
Lawrenceville, Georgia

Adele Fugel
Elementary School Trainer, "Strategies for Teaching Content to
    English Language Learners"
Summer Staff Development
Meadowcreek Elementary School/Gwinnett County Public
    Schools
Lawrenceville, Georgia

About the Authors

Ellen Kottler received her B.A. degree from the University of Michigan, her M.A. degree from Eastern Michigan University, and her Ed.S. degree from the University of Nevada, Las Vegas. She has been a teacher for over 30 years in public and private schools, alternative schools, adult education programs, and universities. She has worked in inner-city schools as well as in suburban and rural settings. She has also worked as a curriculum specialist in charge of secondary social studies and law-related education for one of the country's largest school districts. She is currently a lecturer in the Department of Secondary Education at California State University, Fullerton. Ellen is the coauthor of *Counseling Skills for Teachers* (2000) and *Secrets for Secondary School Teachers: How to Succeed in Your First Year* (1998), also published by Corwin Press.

Jeffrey Kottler received his Ph.D. from the University of Virginia. He is the author of over 40 books in education, counseling, and related fields, including *Succeeding With Difficult Students* (1997), *Travel That Can Change Your Life* (1997), *On Being a Teacher: The Human Dimension* (2000), *Doing Good: Passion and Commitment for Helping Others* (2000), and *Making Changes Last* (2001). Jeffrey is Chair of the Counseling Department at California State University, Fullerton.

Chapter One

Getting to Know
the Student

Michel is a new arrival in your classroom; he has been with you for the past week. While the other children are working on an assignment, you notice that he is intensely occupied looking around the room. Wanting to offer him all the encouragement you can, you approach his desk and ask if he needs any help. At first he looks at you with a blank stare; then he hesitates a moment longer and shakes his head. His eyes move back to the page on his desk in front of him. As soon as you turn your back, his eyes resume their travels around the room.

You sit at your desk bewildered by this interaction. Did he understand what you asked him? Does he have any idea what is going on with the assignment? How are you supposed to help him when you can't even communicate in such a way that he will respond? Does he have some learning disabilities or perhaps some deficit in his social skills? You notice he has yet to interact with the other children. How are you supposed to make any of these determinations when you are not even aware of the extent of his English communication and comprehension?

Sensitivity to Cultural and Linguistic Differences

One American in five speaks a language other than English at home. In particular areas of the country, such as California and Texas, native English speakers are actually outnumbered by those who speak another language at home. This trend can be traced to a number of patterns—shifting populations throughout North America; increased immigration, especially from Latin America and Southeast Asia; and rising birthrates of non-English-proficient or limited-English-proficient populations.

Immigration Patterns

Census Bureau reports indicate that immigration to the United States in the last 20 years has rivaled the rates from the turn of the 20th century. Whereas earlier immigration for the most part came from Europe, newcomers now arrive primarily from Asia, Mexico, and Central and South America. The Hispanic population, for example, is predicted to reach over 40 million by the year 2010, representing 14% of the U.S. population. Likewise, school-age children of Asian background will reach 6% and African Americans will constitute about 16%. In just another 30 years after that, white schoolchildren in the United States will actually be in the minority (Rong, 1998).

If future trends in immigration follow past patterns, it can be expected that the majority of our school-age children will continue to come from Latin America and Asia. Based on figures supplied by the U.S. Department of Immigration and Naturalization Service (1999), newcomers to America arrived most frequently from the following countries in the years 1995-1998:

Rank Order of Top 10 Countries From Where Immigrants Arrive

1. Mexico

2. China

3. India

4. Philippines

5. Dominican Republic

6. Vietnam

7. Cuba

8. Jamaica

9. El Salvador

10. Korea

Based on these same data collected by the Immigration and Naturalization Service (1999), most of these immigrants settled in the following states: California (Los Angeles/Orange County, San Francisco Bay Area), New York (New York City), Florida (Miami), and Texas (Houston), although places such as Boston; Washington, D.C.; and many midwestern cities have also seen an influx of new settlers. It is easy to predict that almost every community will see a significant increase of newcomers from abroad.

New Challenges and Responsibilities

Obviously, some of your students will be members of minority groups who are multilingual in languages other than English; others will have minimal language proficiency, which hinders their ability to be academically or socially successful. Whichever the case, you are going to face increased numbers of students with limited English-speaking ability, adding new challenges to your teaching responsibilities.

As you watch Michel from your desk, you reflect on some of your impressions so far. You have noticed that he smiles when he enters the room. He seems shy and rarely speaks, but you believe that is to be expected, given the new situation he finds himself in. You note that he follows the other children in carrying out routines, yet his schoolwork has been minimal.

When you consider the possible reasons to account for his lack of compliance, you realize that you actually know very little about him. How did he end up where he is? Where did he come from? What is important to him? What does he think about when he is daydreaming? How does he feel inside? You resolve to find some way to get to know him better. In order to carry out an effective plan for any of your students, you will need to assess the skills, abilities, and interests they bring to the classroom, with special attention to their cultural background and language proficiency.

When Teachers Become Students

In the collection of diverse peoples who make up North America, it has become more and more important to be sensitive to individual learning styles, communication patterns, and interaction styles that are reflective of various minority cultures. Thus the approach you might take with a Mexican American student would be quite different from one you would choose with a child from Bosnia or a new arrival from Korea. Before you can ever expect to reach any of the limited-English-speaking children in your class, you must first become a functional expert in their backgrounds. Such a systematic interest will become a foundation from which to structure your teaching efforts.

As one example, a teacher felt frustrated with the lack of progress he had been making with an Inuit child from East Greenland. Not only had the girl failed to develop much proficiency in the English language, but she seemed to manifest serious attention deficit problems and would frequently get out of her seat of her own accord and wander about the room.

Before making a referral to special education or the school psychologist for an assessment, the teacher decided to do a little research on his own. After studying a bit about East Greenlandic culture he realized that the children from her region were rarely given much structure or discipline, because it was believed they carried the spirits of old people and so should be treated with great respect. It was very common for school to be quite "fluid," with children frequently up and about whenever the mood suited them. Furthermore, because Danish was the official language of Greenland and West Greenlandic was the language of instruction in the schools, an East Greenlandic child was already expected to learn three languages in order to function effectively. In some cases, there was considerable resistance to having to learn another one, especially in such a strange world where students were forced to remain still for long periods of time.

Once the teacher had taken the time to learn some background about the cultural origins of this student (and others), he was able to demonstrate much greater understanding and sensitivity to behavior that previously had appeared to him as disruptive, uncooperative, or unmotivated. Language acquisition and proficiency are thus directly related to a student's cultural proficiency, that is, the ability to adapt to the classroom and school environments in such a way that individual needs are recognized and responded to effectively (Lindsey, Nuri Robins, & Terrell, 1999).

Some Problems With Identifying Terms

Before going any farther, it is necessary to address how the student will be described. There has been, and continues to be, much discussion in the field related to selection of a term to identify this population of people who are not native English speakers but who are learning the English language (Cary, 2000). In the first edition of this book, the prevailing term used by teachers to describe children was *English as a second language (ESL) students*. However, for many children, English is not their second language; it is their third, fourth, or one of many languages they are learning. Therefore, ESL is not a fitting label.

As of this writing, the term most commonly used is *English language learners* (ELL). This, too, has its problems, as all children in the United States are learning English. The term *bilingual students* is sometimes used as well, but the problem is that this term implies the students can read, write, and speak in both languages equally. *Language minority* students is another new term that does not work well, because in some areas the number of students learning English will be in the majority. For the purpose of this book, the term *children with limited English* will be used as a way to describe those students whose English is limited in comparison to what would be considered developmentally appropriate for a native English-speaking child with English-speaking parents. This description is meant to be a temporary, not permanent, descriptor and is used to indicate the current language ability of students with no reflection on their potential.

Relationships Are Everything

So much about learning is influenced by the quality of the relationships you develop with students. When kids trust and respect you, when they know you care about them, when they like you and what you stand for, then they will learn almost anything you want to teach (Kottler & Zehm, 2000). Likewise, if students believe teachers are unfair or mean or unduly critical, it is very difficult to make much progress.

Trusting Relationships

Nonnative English speakers may have very good reasons to mistrust the motives of teachers and other authority figures, especially if these professionals are members of the dominant culture. They may have suffered injustices in the past or been subjected to discrimination. They may have heard stories (some true, some exaggerations and distortions) that lead them to be cautious and hesitant.

Yet once teachers develop caring relationships with students, many consequences often follow:

1. Students are willing to take risks without fear of being humiliated.

2. When students are confused or don't understand something, they are more willing to ask for help.

3. Students may be more willing to show caring and respect for one another if the teacher models these same values during daily interactions.

4. Students will be more disclosing about their lives and more honest about their innermost thoughts and feelings when they believe they will be accepted and valued.

The Value of Relationship Skills

Relationship skills are not often taught in teacher preparation programs, which tend to be heavily weighted with emphasis on content areas, curricular issues, technological innovations, and pedagogical methods. Yet there are probably few strategies more powerful and effective in building successful collaborations than those behaviors designed to deepen relationships (Kottler, 2000; Kottler & Kottler, 2000). These include, but are not limited to, the following.

Communicating Constructive Attitudes. Most students (or anyone else for that matter) have a secret fear that they will be judged critically. It is very important to present yourself to students as open, accessible, and nonjudgmental. This means that although you may not approve of certain behaviors that are disruptive or counterproductive, you do not write off the students, as people, just because you don't like their annoying behavior.

Demonstrating Effective "Attending" Behaviors. This means presenting yourself to students as a good listener. You show this through your body posture, eye contact, and facial expressions, communicating your intense interest in what they have to say. It is actually quite rare that anyone gives others their truly undivided attention. Because learning and speaking a language involve far more than merely articulating verbal expression, teachers have the opportunity to model appropriate listening skills in their own behavior.

Asking "Open-Ended Questions." This is the type of query that is designed to foster exploration rather than to cut off communication. Compare, for instance, two questions worded in very different ways:

Closed Question:

Teacher: "So Miguel, did you have a good time with your family this weekend?"

Student: "Sí."

Open Question:

Teacher: "Miguel, what did you do with your family this week-
    end?"

Notice that closed questions can be answered in single-word responses, whereas open questions encourage elaboration. If there is
one mistake that teachers make most often when trying to be helpful, it is in the area of questioning, where they may come across as
interrogating rather than interested.

Listening Actively. Students who are already self-conscious about
their ability to communicate in a new language need lots of reassurance that they have been heard and understood. Demonstrate ways
to listen actively through nonverbal and verbal acknowledgments.
This includes such things as:

1.   Smiling and using facial expressions to communicate inter-
    est and responsiveness
2.   Nodding your head frequently to indicate that you are tracking
3.   Using your body posture to face the person fully and show
    your interest

Reflecting Back What You Heard. One way to prove that you have
not only heard what was said but also understood its deeper meaning is by reflecting back both the content and the underlying feeling
of the message. Note the way the teacher does this with a student
frustrated about a grade on an assignment:

Student: "This grade isn't fair."

Teacher: "You're frustrated because you worked hard on this as-
    signment and you still got what you think is a poor grade."

Student: [nods her head]

Teacher: [waits patiently]

Student: "I spent a lot of time on this. And you still think it
    stinks."

Teacher: "No matter how hard you try, it still seems like it won't make a bit of difference."

In this brief dialogue, the specifics are less important than the very idea that the teacher is trying hard to validate the student's feelings rather than defending herself and her grading policy. She keeps the focus on the student and his feelings, reinforcing his willingness to express himself in English.

Each of these relationship skills is designed to encourage greater communication as well as to help students feel heard and understood. Any of the methods described in the following chapters will work much better if it occurs within a context of constructive, caring relationships.

Understanding the Student's World

The first phase in any helping effort involves learning about the person you are intending to reach. All communication is based on a sensitivity to a person's needs, as well as an understanding of his or her unique world. It is sometimes difficult to fully comprehend what it must be like to live in a place ruled by constant fear of making mistakes.

One student relates his first experience coming to America. He was on a flight from Mexico City to Seattle, his first time ever on an airplane. He was on his way to live with family members who worked as migrant workers in the fruit orchards of the Central Washington Yakima Valley. He didn't speak a word of English.

The boy found himself in a window seat. Rather than feeling privileged and awed by the view of his soon-to-be adopted country out the window, he was feeling increasingly uncomfortable. He had to go to the bathroom very badly, but he was trapped in his seat by the passenger in the aisle seat on his right. He looked over and saw a well-dressed American businessman working diligently on his laptop computer. The boy decided he was some sort of important executive because he wore a suit jacket and a tie that was not even loosened at his neck. He must be working on something very important.

Fearful of interrupting this important man, the boy suffered silently in his seat with his legs crossed. Even if he had wanted to leave his seat to go to the toilet, he had no idea how to ask such a thing in English. He rehearsed, *"Permiso"* and *"Perdoname,"* but it didn't seem right to speak Spanish to such an important man. Instead, this boy recalls that his very first experience on his trip to America was to pee in his pants because he had been too afraid to ask permission to leave his seat. He couldn't communicate even his most basic needs.

It is sometimes hard for us to imagine that anyone could feel so afraid, so ashamed, so reluctant to speak at all, that a student would remain mute. But that is often what nonnative language speakers report is their experience, and until you are able to understand what this is like, you have no chance of ever reaching them.

Before you can ever hope to connect with and influence a child, you must also know about what it is he or she considers most important. This background information involves not only assessing academic skills in verbal or quantitative areas but also learning about family, cultural, and social customs that are an integral part of the child's life.

Here are a number of suggestions for getting to know your students. What makes many of these strategies so helpful is that they do not require a high level of language proficiency to get started.

Take a Picture! You Are Making History

One favorite technique of therapists is to ask new clients during a first interview to show photographs of family members as they are talking about their living situations. This accomplishes several tasks at the same time: (a) It creates an immediate sense of intimacy, because photos reveal one's most important influences; (b) it helps the professional to associate names with faces; and (c) it provides clues as to family relationships that may prove useful when the time comes to understand better what is going on at home.

With limited-English students, photographs provide another advantage in that they don't require much verbal elaboration to have personal meaning. Photographs can be used as an alternative means of communication (although the same images may be interpreted differently based on cultural perceptions). Students may thus be invited to bring in photos that hold particular importance to them or that show individuals who are most significant to them.

In addition, photos can be taken periodically throughout the school year, capturing moments in time. They can be easily displayed. They serve as a reminder to the student of how he or she felt at the beginning of school and how initial impressions and feelings have changed. You can take pictures of the student to record participation in different activities—playing a part in a skit, painting a wall mural, solving a math problem on the board, working on a cooperative learning task, interacting with other children in the lunchroom. Pictures can be taken of projects that are too big to keep on a permanent basis in the classroom.

Pictures are also an excellent way for communicating to parents what happens during the school day. Giving a child a picture of the students and teachers in the classroom will provide him or her with a way to take the events of the school day home to share with parents, other brothers and sisters, extended family, and friends.

One teacher who specializes in working with students from diverse backgrounds explains:

> I think parents feel more comfortable when they see what takes place in school. They are curious about what their child does and with whom he or she spends time. I make sure to indicate the dates the pictures are taken so they can see the progress the child has made over time.

Students can also be invited to bring in pictures of themselves and their family to share with the class. These can be used for get-acquainted activities, to stimulate speech or writing assignments, and to build self-esteem. Most of all, they allow children to help educate others about the unique circumstances in which they live. Among Maori and other indigenous children, for example, their individual names are relatively less important to their families than the mountain and river near where they are from. This, in fact, makes an interesting class activity, in which students are invited to introduce themselves in the Maori way by first talking about the "boat" that brought them to this land (this is a metaphor for their family journey to this time and place), then describing the features of nature that they identify with most strongly, and then finally introducing their family and how it is unique.

The teacher demonstrates this method as follows:

My parents immigrated to this country after World War II. They were Jewish refugees who survived the Holocaust—that is when the Nazis put people of my religion, as well as others, into special camps where they worked as slaves. The boat they arrived on was filled with similar people who were all poor and sick.

After arriving in New York, they made their way to Detroit—that is a city in the Midwest that is known for where they make cars. My river where I come from is called the Detroit River, and there is no mountain nearby, but if I had to choose one, I'd pick Pine Knob, which is a ski hill where I used to play as a child.

My family worked in the automotive factories in a number of different jobs. My last name is of Russian origin and my middle name is Swedish, which is where my mother's family came from.

Obviously, limited-English speakers would have trouble being so detailed in their introductions, so options can be created in which they tell their stories using props, photos, music, and native foods, or even bringing in a family member as a guest.

Although videotaping has some special advantages over still photographs, it presents a few additional problems. Students with limited language proficiency may find it difficult to speak under such "performance" conditions. Until the student is comfortable with the taping process, time in front of the camera should be limited.

Develop a Portfolio

Developing a record of the child's progress in school is an important first step toward getting to know the student. Several resources (MacDonald, 1998; Schurr, 1999) are helpful in guiding your efforts to study systematically a student's performance across a wide range of activities. Make a list of everything the child can do without using language—build, sort, match, categorize, sequence, copy, draw, listen to music, look at pictures, mimic, make faces, pantomime. Then, look for examples of listening, speaking, reading, and writing. If time and opportunity permit, try to observe student behavior in more "natural" settings, because some of the most effective interactions you can ever have with a child are in the hallways (Hazler, 1998).

With respect to using English, notice and categorize mistakes. Are there pronunciation errors, grammatical and syntactical errors, or comprehension and semantic errors? These are to be expected with beginning students. Include notes from your observations of interactions with other people, samples of student work, descriptions of projects, pictures, as well as grades and outside test results you receive.

Determine which instructional activities the student enjoys most. Which activities does the student try to avoid? Could these preferences be a reflection of cultural values? For example, does the student prefer cooperative learning exercises rather than those that require competition? Or does the child prefer to work alone?

Take your explorations one step further and find out what activities the child pursues after school. Is the student a member of a scouting organization, a church group, or an athletic team? Does the student have a pet? Does the student belong to a choir, band, or other school club?

One teacher describes a turning point that occurred with one student she had been struggling to make contact with:

> After a few weeks of digging, I found out he was a soccer player. I went to watch the team play one day after school. The very next time I saw him in class, I started a conversation with him about the game. At first he didn't answer, but I could tell he felt good that I had taken the time to learn about his life. Everything sort of fell into place after that.

What does the child do when he or she is alone? By identifying the child's interests, you can later relate lessons to topics the child will be able to identify with and build on the knowledge base already established.

An eighth-grade teacher shares this example:

I had a young girl who came directly from Mexico the summer before school began. Since she spoke quite well, they put her in a developmental English class . . . mine. She was a good student who was eager to learn, but her grasp of writing English was quite limited. Fragments. No subject-verb agreement. Incorrectly placed modifiers. You get the picture. We spent a lot of time reading, writing, and working on grammar.

In December, the school received tickets to attend the Ballet Folklorico. It was a wonderful evening that all who attended enjoyed. The next day, the assignment was to write about the experience from the previous evening. When she called me over to read her rough draft, I was moved to tears. It was the most beautifully written memory I had read, and it was perfectly punctuated! An English teacher's dream. I learned that to truly get the best from one's students, teachers must make the assignments meaningful so that students want to show off what the teacher has helped them learn.

Not only will a portfolio provide a structure for tracking student experiences and progress, but it will give you a well-rounded picture of the student. Portfolio assessment will also give you a wide variety of material to present at parent conferences. You will also be able to provide the student with a visual record of his or her progress.

Explore the Student's Family Background

To learn about the student's family background, plan information-seeking activities. For example, through geography lessons you can discover where students came from, whether it was a rural or urban setting, and the length of time they have spent in this country.

During one-on-one conversations you may learn a lot more about why the family immigrated to North America in the first place. Was it for better economic opportunities? Were they escaping some sort of persecution or physical threats? Of course, you would wish to be very sensitive in the way you approach this subject, because there may be shame, guilt, or legal problems associated with the immigration.

When one of us (Jeffrey) was teaching a university honors seminar, he discovered that more than half the class had been in this country for less than 10 years. But what was really surprising was the number of students who had suffered terribly in their countries of origin. Several students escaped abject poverty. One Cambodian student had watched her family murdered before her eyes. Several others narrowly escaped life-threatening incidents, and all of these early experiences significantly affected their learning in school and mastery of their new language. Because all of these students were high achievers, they had actually demonstrated tremendous resilience as a result of early traumas. They reported that their teachers made a huge difference in helping them put the past behind them and channel their energies toward productive directions. Many of their siblings had not been nearly so fortunate.

Through the use of pictures, as mentioned earlier, you can find out how many brothers and sisters are in the family, their ages and sexes, whether they attend school or not, and whether extended family members live in the household. Through conversation you can learn the lines of authority in the family and the patterns of socialization.

On the elementary school level, this information can be elicited through discussion of the family, counting and sorting activities, or responses to children's literature. On the secondary level, the information can be collected through discussion of immigration in a social studies class, the family in a home economics class, genetics in a science class, the concept of role in a sociology class, or reaction to a reading in an English class. Lessons on multicultural topics such as relationships, legends, customs, power, and authority can be incorporated into the curriculum.

Once students develop some degree of rudimentary writing skills, they can express their ideas through writing assignments such as journals, autobiographies, or structured worksheets. Those who are not yet proficient in their writing can instead draw pictures to respond to questions or express themselves. One of the best assignments for any age group, also favored by counselors and therapists who are attempting to learn about children's experiences, is to ask them to draw a picture of themselves with their family. Through words, gestures, dramatic enactments, or further drawings, they can then be encouraged to talk about their family.

Learning about the student's position in the family and assigned household responsibilities will give you insight into behavior at school and after school. Does the child care for younger brothers and sisters or elderly grandparents? Does the child cook and clean for the family? Does the child work to support the family? These responsibilities will limit the student's involvement in school as well as in community activities. For example, the student may not have time or money to come to a spaghetti dinner, talent show, or extracurricular activities. However, you will become aware of the students who are capable of fulfilling leadership roles, those who are nurturing, and those who are capable of taking on tasks requiring responsibility in the classroom.

In the example that began this chapter, Michel disclosed, through gestures and halting English, that he was left alone much of the time. His parents both worked long hours, leaving him to take care of the house. He was able to communicate that he did understand much of what was said to him. He had been watching a lot of television, especially music videos, and he found that by memorizing the words to the songs, his ear was becoming more accustomed to English. He very much wanted to do his homework, but he was just too busy with things that he had to do around the house. In his spare time, what little he could find, he had started playing around with a harmonica. Music seemed to be an important part of his life.

Exploring the area of home responsibilities will also give you an arena in which to converse with the child, to give him or her an opportunity to practice speaking English in a private setting with you. Just think about how self-conscious you might feel using your limited proficiency in another language when speaking with native speakers in their country. Children may thus be more willing to try out their own limited English if they trust you and feel that you are not judging them harshly because of their feelings of ineptitude.

Furthermore, the child has the opportunity to show off what he or she is most proud of—baby sister, new puppy, knowledge of his or her native history, cooking skills, or harmonica playing. This can later be shared with the class in small groups or even in the whole community as confidence grows.

Determine the Home Attitude Toward Learning English

Find out how many people at home speak English in order to have some idea of support available. If nobody else in the home speaks

English well, that may guide your efforts to develop alternative support systems that can provide assistance with schoolwork and language development.

It is also important to find out what the attitude is among family members toward learning English. In two different Arab American families, for example, quite different messages were given at home. In one case, the child's entire family was attempting to learn English together; the whole process of learning English became a fun, challenging activity that brought them closer together. The family watched situation comedies on television at night and tried to talk about what happened in English. The child in this situation received a strong message from his parents: If you want to succeed in this country you must speak English perfectly.

In another case, the family atmosphere emphasized much more the importance of maintaining their cultural roots. Arabic was the only language encouraged at home. Because the parents both lived and worked in an exclusively Arab community, English remained a "foreign" language. In fact, it was entirely possible for members of this community to live their whole lives speaking only their native language. The message thus communicated to the child was: Speak English only if you must, but Arabic is your real tongue.

It is not uncommon for first-generation immigrants to feel that learning English is not important and to resent the new language and customs of the United States. Second-generation immigrants may also feel that their parents have been successful without learning English and that there is no reason for them to be any different. If they are from a community where others speak their language, they prefer to speak in the language with which they feel most comfortable, the first language. Even at school, language opportunities in English can be mostly avoided.

Many new immigrants have left behind all that is familiar; all they have remaining is their own language. As in the case of the first Arab American example, others may see speaking English as a vital survival skill and refuse to speak native languages in the home. This, of course, presents its own problems, because then the children may lose much of their ethnic heritage. They may experience internal conflicts, loss of cultural identity, and marginalization among those of their own background (Robinson & Howard-Hamilton, 2000).

There are certain tribes of Native Americans, for example, in which there is no longer anyone who speaks the native language. The children have lost the opportunity to connect with their past even if they wanted to. Among a band of Paiute Indians in our local area, one child expressed an interest in learning his native dialect. Unfortunately, there was nobody within the group who remembered enough of the language to teach it.

Investigate the Nature of Past School Experiences

Another factor to consider in your assessment is the type of school background the students have. Some children may have experienced an authoritarian style with an emphasis on memorization and recitation. They may be used to large-group instruction with an emphasis on oral communication. They may have learned to adopt passive learning roles. The grading system and grading scales may be different than the ones used in North America. Consequently, they may experience difficulty adjusting to different expectations for behavior in school. These children may be uncomfortable working in groups and often choose not to actively participate unless directed. One of us (Jeffrey), for example, works with groups of teachers and counselors in Hong Kong in which the only people who will speak up in class are those who are perfectly fluent and confident in English. They are so afraid of making a mistake and losing face that most prefer not to say anything at all. To complicate matters, cultural values emphasize a hierarchy of status based on age rather than experience. Thus younger students, who may have a wealth of experience in the classroom, will defer to older classmates who have never taught before. This is just one example of the ways that any student's behavior must be examined within a particular cultural context.

Determine the Stage of Acculturation

Children will develop different attitudes toward learning English based on how long they have been in the country and where they fall in the *continuum of acculturation,* a concept that describes the process by which members of minority groups become socialized into accepting the values of the dominant culture (Berry & Sam, 1997). Although the progression through the process of acculturation varies from individual to individual, several stages have been identified

(Atkinson, Morten, & Sue, 1997). At first children may be quite excited. Everything is novel. Each day is a new experience. Then the students experience culture shock. Students feel frustrated by their efforts as they begin to adapt to the ways of the new culture. In the next stage, students ideally gain more control and are more successful. They begin to adjust to school, and English language skills improve rapidly. In the final stage students fully adjust to the new culture, ideally retaining their close association to their family and cultural roots.

The ease with which children move through the stages depends on the amount of contrast between cultures and the amount of discrimination faced by their cultural group. Family factors include the reasons for immigration, the degree of separation from the family, and the disruption of economic status. Personal factors include the age of the child, gender, language fluency, attitudes and personality characteristics, and the nature of prior formal education. Younger children have an easier time than adolescents, as they have had less opportunity for their native cultural values, beliefs, and customs to become embedded. Females from developing nations are likely to pursue domestic responsibilities rather than higher education. Students who develop communication skills, exhibit flexibility, and can build relationships will be able to adapt more quickly than those who do not. Positive attitudes toward education and the new culture as well as an openness to new ideas are associated with acculturation. Personality characteristics such as patience, tolerance, self-confidence, and healthy self-esteem open the door, whereas perfectionism, rigidity, and self-centeredness make it difficult to adjust. Teachers are encouraged to see children as individuals and to be sensitive to the cultural values related to education, gender, and assimilation that students bring to the classroom.

Invite Parents to Participate in Your Class

As mentioned previously, one useful strategy is to invite the parent to give a special presentation in class related to his or her culture. Every child wants to feel that his or her parent is important enough to be invited to the classroom. There are other ways to involve the parent, such as asking him or her to volunteer to help supervise a special activity (such as an art project or science experiment). Many would welcome an invitation to chaperone a field trip. They can also read to students in the native language to help develop literacy skills. Having native English-speaking students be a part of the reading group will give them a sense of what it is like to be surrounded by a language with which they are not familiar. It also shows that there is a place for diverse languages in the classroom. Time given to training volunteer parents should be well worth the effort.

Pay Attention to Social and Cultural Customs

It is important to become aware of individual and cultural differences and how they may contribute to potential problems in the classroom through miscommunication. Doing an ethnographic study of your students will provide you with a wealth of information explaining their behavior and will give you insight into how best to help them in the classroom. Individuals differ on the following dimensions:

- Verbal communication (pronunciation, patterns of speech, tempo of speech, stress, and pitch)

- Nonverbal communication (eye contact, meaning of gestures)

- Proxemics (spatial distance between people; e.g., some people like to stand very close to one another, and backing away from them would be taken as an affront)

- Interpersonal touching (e.g., whether the student prefers a light or firm pat on the back)

- Attention span (ability and motivation to sustain interest)

- Orientation toward learning (e.g., preference for a quiet or noisy background)

- Social values (peer group influences)

- Intellectual orientation (e.g., is frequent questioning valued or discouraged?)

In considering the social and cultural background of your students, ask yourself the following questions:

1. Has the student been socialized to be an active participant or a passive recipient of information in the classroom?

2. How is the concept of time viewed? Is punctuality a virtue, or is time considered to be flexible?

3. Are students expected to make eye contact with their teachers or to look down out of respect?

4. Do students nod their heads to be polite or to show they understand?

5. Do parents regard teachers as experts and refrain from expressing differences of opinion?

6. Is cooperation or competition encouraged?

7. Is the family patriarchal, restricting educational aspirations for female children?

8. Is education or work valued more in the family?

9. Do students expect specific directions for carrying out tasks and therefore have difficulty choosing their own learning activities?

10. Do students not ask questions because they have been taught not to bother adults?

11. Is the student expected to tell the teacher what the teacher wants to hear (e.g., that an assignment was completed when it hasn't even been started)?

12. Are expressions of emotions and feelings emphasized or hidden?

13. Are speaking or listening modes of communication preferred?

14. Do students exhibit low self-esteem and self-defeating behaviors because they feel they cannot succeed as a result of socioeconomic marginality and discrimination?

15. Is change considered inevitable and desirable, or is tradition revered?

In order to understand parent reactions and avoid misunderstanding or miscommunication, it is critical for the teacher to learn about the specific background of the student. As Allington and Cunningham (1996) point out as one example, some parents may not understand the difference between books that are assigned as texts throughout the year and given to the student versus library books, which are "borrowed" and must be returned in a few weeks.

Scarcella (1990) encourages teachers to compare the values promoted by the mainstream middle class to those of other cultures. Values in the United States include such things as organized time, competitiveness and upward mobility, equality of opportunity, individualism, autonomy, and informality. Of course, even within the diverse regions of the United States, we can see huge differences between values on the East Coast versus the West Coast; between the North and the South; between midwestern rural areas versus urban areas; and between individual states such as Texas, California, Vermont, Mississippi, and Alaska.

One of the most common mistakes that beginners often make is forgetting that the differences within cultural groups can be greater than those between them. One can as easily get in trouble by making generalizations about people based on their cultural identity as by ignorance of knowing anything at all.

Each major cultural group, be it Asian or Latino, has differences in its subgroups, and cultures are always evolving. There are also differences in children due to the education and socioeconomic background of the parents as well as the length of time and nature of experience spent in the United States. As people become acculturated to their specific environment in the United States, they take on new values. For this reason, it is important to investigate the background of each student.

If we contrast just a few cultural groups that are strongly represented in schools today, Chinese emphasize obedience, respect for elders, family centeredness, emotional control, and parents strongly involved with education. It is interesting to note the difference in English proficiency among the various subgroups. Hong Kong Chinese who have been educated privately are often fluent, whereas those who attended public schools may have greater difficulty speaking and even more problems writing. In mainland China and Taiwan, English is offered beginning at the middle school level, but the quality of instruction may be poor.

In Filipino culture, values emphasize respect for elders and education as a means of improving socioeconomic status. English is offered in the first year of school and is the language of instruction.

Koreans also have a strong respect for elders, values of hard work, traditional family roles, family centeredness, cooperation, and interdependence. English is required in junior high and high school with an emphasis on grammar rather than pronunciation.

Mexican values include respect for authority, achievement, and pride in heritage. Puerto Rican culture values family centeredness, individualism, dignity of the individual, and bilingualism.

Students will learn that certain behaviors are appropriate for school and others are expected at home, just as they learn that certain speech is acceptable on the street but not in the classroom. However, they may get confused as to what to do or say in a given situation. Often students will develop two codes of conduct. One story in particular makes this point clear. A young boy was being disciplined by his mother. She had been very unhappy with something that he did. After she finished scolding him, he looked at her and said, "Am I supposed to look at you [as teachers at school request] or look away from you [as a sign of respect]? I can't remember."

Teachers must realize, too, that students will respond in very different ways to the pull between their two cultures. Some are eager and proud to adopt the new ways, whereas others are resentful and resistant.

You will find it valuable to learn about the cultural characteristics particular to your students. In some ways, this is the best part of your job—that you have the opportunity to learn not only from books but from the fascinating people you work with. Teachers must be aware of cultural differences in order to create a supportive environment. Facial expressions and gestures can be widely interpreted—even a smile can have different interpretations, from loving to cynical.

Just as you do not wish to misinterpret what your students' behavior means, neither do you want them to misread your gestures and actions. Discussing communication patterns—both verbal and nonverbal—with all your students will help everyone develop a sensitivity to differences and similarities.

Suggested Activities

1. Identify the limited-English speakers in your classroom. Develop a list of interview questions you would like to ask their parents related to student behavior.

2. Identify the values that you promote in your classroom. Compare this list to the values held by the students in your classroom from different backgrounds.

3. Observe a limited-English speaker in your classroom. Note how that child interacts with others in school—students, cafeteria staff, the principal, other teachers. Use this information to plan activities that will build on the student's strengths.

4. Reflect on times in your own educational experience when you felt mute, alienated, or isolated. Talk about these experiences in a small group of friends or classmates. Discuss what the common factors were that most contributed to your discomfort. Find a consensus as to what helped you the most to come out of your shell.

Chapter Two

Establishing a Comfortable Environment

Once a working relationship has been established with students to the point that you have gotten to know a bit about one another, the next step is to create and maintain the sort of classroom environment that will be safe, productive, and supportive. In the case of Michel, for instance, you might ask yourself several questions while considering this task: What can I do to help Michel feel more comfortable in the classroom? How can I structure the learning environment to facilitate his development of English as well as his mastery of the material in my curriculum? Just as important, how can I help him to like being at school, at least during the time that he is with me?

A Welcoming Environment

Encourage a new student to come into the classroom with gentle but not overbearing enthusiasm. It cannot be overemphasized how important it is to learn to pronounce the student's name correctly. One student reports what a tremendous difference such an effort made to him:

> My name, Efraim, is difficult for many Anglos to get right. I don't make a big deal about it one way or another, but when I first came to this country, my teacher made me say my name over and over until she could say it perfectly. She used to kid me that this was going to be her final examination and that I had her permission to correct her if she ever made a mistake. I can't tell you how much I appreciated that effort on her part. I really trusted her.

When Jeffrey was teaching in Iceland, the single most important thing he did to win students' trust and respect was to insist on pronouncing their names in their Native language even though most were willing to allow him the use of an Americanized derivative. Because Icelandic is one of the most difficult languages in the world to pronounce, this meant devoting literally dozens of hours to practice listening to recordings he made of the students pronouncing their own names coupled with their photographs. The message came through strongly that because he was willing to work so hard to learn something about their language, they should overcome their own inhibitions about speaking in English (the language of instruction for these classes). As is so often the case, their actual proficiency in the language far exceeded their confidence levels.

It also helps if you can learn a few phrases in the student's native language, so that you can greet him or her each day with a special welcome: *Ka hue?* ("What's happening?" in Fijian); *Apa khabar?* ("How are you?" in Malaysian); *Gracias por hacer un esferuzo*

("Thank you for making an effort" in Spanish); *Seu trabalho e excelente* ("Your work is excellent" in Portuguese). Reaching out to students in this way may be the most important thing you do.

Look for clues in the student's behavior as to what will make him or her feel most comfortable. Does the student cling to your side or stand independently away? Does the student speak freely or just give a nod of the head? Do you need to assign a partner to stay with the child for a few days and guide him or her through the myriad of school day activities?

Picture yourself in the child's position—what would help *you* to feel more at ease in the school? Imagine that you are living in a strange, new place where almost everything familiar to you is now gone. You don't understand the rules, can't comprehend what people are saying around you, and can't even ask for the things you need most. You feel scared, lonely, and lost. Now, get outside your own skin and crawl into the child. Based on what you already know and understand about his or her experience, background, and personality, what might make the most difference?

Modeling Risk Taking

It is interesting that teachers are so eager for students to take constructive risks with their learning, but we often show the same reluctance to do so. We also play it safe and embrace caution because we don't want to make a mistake or appear clueless. One of the misconceptions that some teachers hold is that if you can't get it right the first time, you should wait until you can select the perfect intervention. This is not only inhibiting but inadvisable.

In school we often learned that when faced with questions, there were only four multiple choices, one of which was correct and the others wrong. Success was simply a matter of selecting the correct option from among those presented. Then we get out into the real world, where not only are the choices limitless, but there is often no way to figure out which is the correct one. In any given situation, there are a dozen different things you could do or say, any of which might work fairly well. Even after the episode is over, it is still nearly impossible to figure out if your intervention was the best alternative.

The good news, however, is that it often doesn't matter so much if what you did was perfectly effective or the absolute best intervention. If you can develop a trusting, respectful relationship with your students, they will give you the benefit of the doubt when you mess up or make mistakes. Also, if you are willing to model taking risks, as well as owning your misjudgments, you make it much easier for students to do the same.

Your job is to provide students with a comfortable space to sit and work and the supplies necessary to complete their assignments. You can do this by eliminating distractions as much as possible. Introduce the child to a few of the other students at a time. Help him or her learn to pronounce the names of other classmates, and have them practice the new child's name. Be sure to continue eye contact and gestures of reassurance throughout the day. Provide support as often as possible. Do whatever you can to make your classroom feel like a safe place for learning; for making mistakes; and for experimenting with new, more effective ways of communicating.

Introduce Labels

To help students develop their English skills, label items in your room with name cards. Create safety signs using pictures. Label supply closets with pictures and names of objects. Have dictionaries readily available, and use them often yourself to model for the children. Make time for the new student to teach classmates about the names of things in his or her own language. In this way there is a cultural exchange, and the limited-English speaker feels valued. You will also end up introducing all your students to a world of different cultures and languages that will only make them more adaptable after they leave school.

In one classroom, the teacher took inventory of all the languages that students spoke at home, numbering close to a dozen. She then made up signs of the most common features of the room and had the students insert the word in their native languages. Next to the light switch, for example, was a sign that read "Luces," "Lumières," "Luci," "Lichter," proclaiming in Spanish, French, Italian, German, and many other tongues what was located in this spot. Not only did this give helpful directions, but it also communicated respect for many different ways of saying the same thing.

Use Multicultural Materials in the Classroom

Hang up posters reflecting the diversity of people and customs in our society. Communicate to others by the way you design your space that differences are valued. For example, display different alphabets used around the world. Pictures of people's faces from around the world can also be represented. One teacher reveals a favorite strategy:

> I always put up a map of the world and have my students indicate with a pushpin where they are from. I find even the native English speakers have come from different states and like to identify where they were born.

As this teacher implies, cultural diversity is not only represented in one's country of origin, but also in the particular geographical region where one's family might have come from. Clearly, students from Texas, New York, Hawaii, or Mississippi also speak different dialects and embrace different cultural customs.

Feature the accomplishments of people from different backgrounds. Play different kinds of music. Select posters that reflect different styles of art from around the world. Bring speakers to the classroom to talk about their cultures so that students will become familiar with a variety of customs—not only clothing and food but also mannerisms and values. Often the students' relatives will be happy to bring artifacts from home and share their personal stories with the class. Read stories from different cultures. Identify concepts around which to plan a multicultural curriculum for the classroom so that students will be able to view the world around them from diverse ethnic perspectives.

Connect With Native Language Speakers

Find out if there are other children who speak the same language, if not in the classroom then somewhere in the school. One teacher suggests,

> An effective strategy I have used with my English language learner class is checking for understanding. I use a student who does understand at least some English to speak in their common

language to make sure the non-English-speaking student does understand a word or phrase.

These student helpers can explain procedures and answer questions. They can offer emotional support by identifying with the experiences of the new student. Furthermore, they can serve as role models. Contact bilingual adults to work with you and the student. Contact the English language learner teacher in your area to come and welcome the new student and to provide an orientation to your school.

Among members of some cultural groups, parents and children are used to thinking of school as an extension of home. Not only would bilingual adults be delighted to help out, but they might even feel disappointed when *not* invited to participate in the educational process. In one Aboriginal school on a reservation in Northern Queensland (Australia), the principal and teachers canvassed the whole surrounding community to make sure that everyone understood that the school *belonged* to all of them; it was just as much their home as a place where their children visited. Before long, parents and other adults began visiting the classrooms in the beginning, mostly as observers, and then later they were put to work according to their interests and abilities. One interesting sidelight is that there were no longer any discipline problems in the school because there was always some neighbor or family member on campus to make certain that children acted in respectful, appropriate ways. Once efforts were made to make the school familiar rather than foreign territory, the students made significant progress.

Give Recognition Where It Is Due

It is important to recognize the efforts that children make, but this is especially so for those who are struggling the most. Our attention is often so drawn to problems that we forget to notice incremental improvement, especially in those who are having the most difficulty.

It is generally a good idea to find as many ways and excuses as possible to provide support, reinforcement, and encouragement. Efforts should be made to introduce such recognition in a natural rather than a contrived way. There is nothing more shameful than to realize that a teacher is rewarding you for some token gesture that did not really involve much effort.

Set Routines

Students new to North America may need to learn how to "do" school. Establish routines throughout the day and review them with the class. The children with limited English are usually quick to follow the lead of others. With older students, make out a schedule for them to follow. Be conscious of your terminology. Use the same wording from day to day. Rather than say "It's time for gym" one day and "It's time for PE" the next, choose one term and stick with it. Indicate with gestures the directions in which to move. Demonstrate with objects. Write important words on the board or display them on an overhead projector. Ask other students to model responses for your limited-English-speaking students.

Fostering Classroom Involvement

In addition to strategies designed to build relationships with students and to help them develop rudimentary English skills, much can also be initiated within the classroom to make assimilation easier.

Assign a Buddy

As we mentioned previously, it is often helpful to assign students to be "buddies" or helpers. One classmate can be responsible for helping with schoolwork. Another can be responsible for guiding the student to lunch. A third can be responsible for identifying the correct bus for the ride home after school. These initial contacts often lead to friendships in which the child must learn to speak better English in order to communicate.

In particular, a study partner will be useful in showing the student what materials to use, demonstrating procedures, and reexplaining information in "student" language. The partner can read to the child and work with the student orally until literacy skills develop. The partner will model social customs appropriate to the classroom. In return, the partner has the opportunity to develop responsibility and leadership skills. In fact, in the optimal classroom environment, children compete for the privilege of guiding the newcomer. One teacher explains:

> I always assign a buddy to each of my English language learners. Children love to help and it makes them feel important to help others. The buddies feel proud of their contributions to the classroom and often make new friends as well.

Small Groups

As the comfort level rises, the nature of the student's participation in the classroom can change to that of cooperative groups. The small-group setting may actually be more consistent with the child's cultural background than the whole-class setting. Small groups will give the student exposure to additional peers, provide for hearing different points of view (as well as accents), and enable him or her to contribute to a project. The student will have the opportunity to try out new language skills with peers as an audience before facing the teacher.

"I think small groups are less threatening to children," one teacher admits before continuing:

> Children often fear they will be laughed at if they make a mistake. They don't want to be ridiculed in front of a big audience. In small groups they can make contributions in various ways without needing to use a lot of language. They can be a timer, an artist, an encourager, or the supplies captain. Also, they hear "kid talk" rather than "teacher talk," which is probably the language they are more interested in learning.

In one school, a teacher adapted some of the activities from "adventure-based" interventions so that limited-English-speaking students were mixed with other children and then given group assignments that were essentially nonverbal—cooperating in such a way as to get everyone through an obstacle course; to take turns catching one another during "trust falls"; and to do group "juggling," in which the children work to get as many balls into play as possible.

Because I (Jeffrey) do a lot of teaching abroad, especially in countries where English is the third language, I have evolved routines in which I do most of the classroom work in cooperative groups in which students can help one another with the assignments in a mix of languages. In my last class in Hong Kong, there was a Hawaiian student who spoke little Chinese and several Chinese students who were very apprehensive about their English skills. However, once paired together in the same group, they were all able to help one another from their respective strengths.

Whole Group

Following individual conversations with you and practice with groups of students, the limited-English child should be ready to speak in front of the entire class. Nevertheless, careful thought must be given as to the type of response you will ask for, depending on the language proficiency of the child. A nod or shake of the head, indicating "Yes" or "No," may be the only response the child is capable of. Later, a child may be deliberately prepared to answer one particular question at a future time: "OK, Michel, tomorrow during math I am going to ask for a volunteer to tell us what is most similar between two different sets of numbers. Now, what are you going to say?"

In order to build confidence and skills incrementally, it is often helpful to conduct such rehearsals with children who are particularly anxious or hesitant. If time permits, you can even role-play situations that are predicted to occur next. For instance, "Nadya, when you go to the cafeteria next hour and stand in line for lunch, let's say that instead of pointing to what you want to order, you ask for it. How will you say what you want? Pretend I am the person standing behind the counter."

Learning English as a second language takes a long time. Students will be able to understand long before they are able to speak. There may be a silent period in which the student learns by listening but is ready to speak. Language acquisition will be more effective if what the student hears is comprehensible. The learning will be facilitated by your conscious incorporation of strategies such as use of gestures, visual aids, regalia, and repetition. In response, the student can demonstrate comprehension by using gestures or pointing to pictures. You can also ask students to "act out" a response to a question.

Structured Responses

For many children, speaking in front of a group of people, especially one including an adult in an authority position, can be a terrifying experience. Carefully wording questions to call for a "yes" or "no" response or providing a choice of words for the student to choose from will make it easy for a student just beginning to learn English. Later, open-ended questions can generate more extensive answers. As mentioned previously, students can practice with partners or in a small group before giving a response in front of the entire class. It is important to extend your *wait time,* the amount of time you allow a student to formulate and give a response. Children with limited English often just need a little more time. Your patience and your students' patience will be appreciated. The next chapter will discuss the stages of language acquisition and what kind of responses you as a teacher can expect.

Meeting the Families

Getting to know students means knowing their families. All behavior occurs not only within a cultural context but also within a unique family environment. Based on what is called "systems" theory, teachers are encouraged to look at all individual behavior within a much larger perspective. If a student is having trouble in school, these problems may very well be the result of things going on at home. Likewise, the child's behavior influences the actions of others within the family. Because the classroom and school are also human systems, the same thing is true there as well: Each person's behavior is both the cause and effect of the behavior of others within the community.

It is for this reason that some teachers and many counselors are inclined to think in "systemic" terms whenever they encounter difficulties, asking questions such as the following:

1. What is this student's behavior really saying?

2. Who is the student possibly helping or enabling as a result of maintaining the status quo?

3. What would be the influence and impact of change for this student?

4. What "benefits" is this student enjoying as a result of remaining stuck?

5. What is the particular meaning of this behavior in light of the student's family history and current situation?

Imagine, for example, that a student you know is quite bright and capable makes only meager progress in learning and applying English proficiency in school. Because the student already speaks fluent French in addition to several different dialects of her native Cambodia, you know she is quite capable in language development, yet for some reason she does not seem to be learning, or at least using, much English in her daily interactions.

Upon investigating further, you discover that her parents are having relationship problems at home, threatening divorce. As long as their child is struggling in school, the parents are remaining together for the sake of family stability. In their culture, doing well in school is the only measure of success in their new country. That their child is doing so poorly is a source of great shame and anguish to all of them, but ironically, it is the glue that is keeping the family intact. The consequences of the child's improving significantly might very well be the parents' splitting up, so the child is actually functioning as a stabilizing factor.

It is often so important to build bridges with families and parents so as to better understand the larger context for the student's behavior as well as to structure interventions that involve the whole family (Montgomery, 1999). After all, it is one of teachers' greatest sources of frustration that we can do our jobs so well in school, and then everything can be undone once the students leave our influence. This is especially the case if children live in communities or homes that directly or indirectly sabotage school performance.

There will be several occasions for meeting with parents of your students—open house at school; parent conferences; and other school events such as field days, recitals, and award ceremonies. Generally speaking, it is a principle of systemic intervention that the more participants you get involved in the change process, the more likely you are to influence the whole system in an enduring way. This could very well mean that with some "parent" conferences it might be entirely appropriate to invite grandparents and other extended family members as well.

Opening Lines of Communication

To prepare for the school encounters, you can send explanatory letters home, provided they are in the parents' native language and the parents can read. A telephone call from someone who speaks the native language will also acquaint the parents with the customs of the school. Some parents will not be able to come to school if there are younger children in the home. You will have to inform them if baby-sitting is available or if they will be welcome to bring the younger children with them. Transportation may also be a problem. Arranging for rides with a neighbor or a parent volunteer would be helpful.

Be aware that to parents from some cultures, a letter or call from school can be a source of embarrassment. These parents feel it is their responsibility to teach their children how to behave. Any request from the school may be misinterpreted as a failure on their part. Such situations can be avoided if the teacher, or another parent, can explain the importance of parent-teacher communication and the school emphasis on involving parents in the educational process through regular conferences.

Conferences

There are several things to keep in mind when conducting parent conferences (see Kottler & Kottler, 2000; Lawrence & Hunter, 1995). Greeting the parents by name with the correct pronunciation will make a positive first impression. Allow plenty of time. Let the parents look around the room and familiarize themselves with the setting. Inform the parents that conferences are requested on a regular basis as school policy. Encourage the parents to talk about their child by asking questions:

- What is the child's behavior like at home?

- What were the child's past educational experiences like?

- Does the child mention any problems or difficult situations?

- Is the child or any member(s) of the family experiencing any cultural conflicts?

- What are the parents' or guardians' goals for the child with respect to education?

- Are there any special needs or customs you need to take into consideration?

If the parent or guardian is not able to communicate, a family member or friend can help mediate the conversation.

Grading scales and testing measures may not be familiar to parents. Reports that have been sent home from school may be ignored or misinterpreted. Much attention has been placed on testing of late, and it will be helpful to explain the purpose and importance of criterion-based tests and norm-referenced tests particular to your school district. You may also want to present the importance of homework as a supplement to class instruction to the parents.

One way in which schools in the United States differ from schools in other parts of the world is in extracurricular activities. From clubs and enrichment classes in art, dance, and music to athletics, native English-speaking children have many choices of activities from the time they leave school in the afternoon through the early evening. It is important to explain the importance of these activities to all parents, as they are not included in the school curriculum.

In light of the values of various groups presented previously, it follows that parents will have different assumptions as to the role of the teacher in their child's education. For example, Asian parents often expect a formal atmosphere and strict discipline in the classroom. They see the teacher as the authority and therefore may not understand the purpose of such activities as learning centers and writing workshops until these are explained. Rote memorization and observation are activities with which they are familiar. They would expect emphasis on the basics, and they will be uncomfortable making decisions about their child's welfare, being accustomed to deferring to the professional educator. Rather than viewing Asian parents as uncaring, a teacher who is familiar with the values of the culture will be able to see such responses as respectful or deferential and avoid misinterpretation.

It is also helpful to collect samples of the student's work to present to the parents to show their child's progress. Pictures of the student involved in various activities will also provide information to parents as to how the time in school is spent. You can involve the student in the conference to explain, in the language the parents best understand, the accomplishments made up to this point, how the student is evaluated, and goals identified for the future.

By developing your sensitivity to the socially appropriate customs related to interpersonal relations of the home culture, you will begin to build bridges that will further aid the work you are doing with the children. You will be able to recruit parents as partners in developing mutually agreed-on goals for the students.

Teaching is about developing relationships with children, regardless of the way communication is initiated. The better you get to know the limited-English child, the more able you are to relate to him or her in language that is accessible. What greater gift can we offer children than the opportunity to improve their ability to express themselves?

Suggested Activities

1. Reflect on (or discuss in class or small groups) those factors that made classrooms most and least comfortable for you. What did teachers do that made you feel most likely to become actively involved in activities? What did teachers do that inhibited you most?

2. Develop a number of activities that you could use in your classroom appropriate for (a) paired, (b) small-group, and (c) whole-group lessons.

3. Brainstorm ways to create a multicultural environment in the classroom.

4. In small groups, talk about a time when, although you were knowledgeable and educated about a subject, you felt mute and couldn't communicate effectively. Share what it would be like to feel that way almost all the time.

5. Role-play a parent conference representing several of the cultural groups that you are most likely to encounter in your classroom.

Chapter Three

Understanding Second-Language Development

I n order to use many of the methods presented in the previous and subsequent chapters, it is necessary to have some background in the nature of language acquisition. At the very least, you must have some notion about how children develop second-language abilities. In addition, you will need to have some idea about how long this process usually takes and what you can do to help facilitate development.

With students who speak limited English who are placed in your classroom for all or part of the day, your task becomes twofold: to teach the curriculum required by your school district and to provide language instruction in English. By becoming aware of the principles related to second-language development, you will be able to plan for the integration of content and language skills so that your students will learn to use English as they interact with each other and become involved in the academic experiences you structure for them.

Second-Language Principles

There are a number of principles that operate in the process of learning a second language. Many of these, such as the contextual nature of words—how their meaning depends on the specific situation—are a part of what teachers already understand. For example, a *party* can refer to a political group organized to promote a political platform and support its candidates, not only to a festive occasion where one eats cake and ice cream. However, other principles that emphasize social and cultural factors are not so readily apparent without some review of the underlying concepts.

Language Learning and Language Acquisition

There is a difference, as Krashen (1996) has pointed out, between learning a language and acquiring one. The latter occurs informally as children subconsciously develop language skills by listening to others and becoming aware of language in their surroundings. This "inside-out" process takes place as students participate in their environment.

Language development also occurs in formal settings, such as when adults consciously develop language skills by attending school, listening to tapes, or hiring private tutors. This "outside-in" process takes place in structured situations and, as we well know, is considerably less inspiring as an environment for developing fluency.

Because the object of language is meaningful communication, the emphasis today on teaching English to speakers of other languages is to promote second-language development in settings in which students will *acquire* the target language. As such, the goal is to provide social interactions for students in which they will create meaningful communication in English as they develop academically.

As an example, you may recall situations in a foreign land in which you absolutely had to communicate in order to find a bathroom or get directions back to your hotel. Under these desperate circumstances, we are often amazed at how quickly we can acquire the necessary verbal (and nonverbal) skills to get our needs met. The object of our educational efforts is to structure just such situations for students, in which they acquire English as a means for survival or in a way that is useful in accomplishing a task, rather than as another in a series of homework assignments.

Appropriate Level of Communication

In order to foster development of English, you as the teacher must provide communication that can be understood. This should include words that students already understand plus new vocabulary that they will be able to figure out from the context in which it is presented. If the student is able to understand what you are trying to communicate, then you have created what Krashen (1996) refers to as "comprehensible input." For example, a teacher addresses a child as follows: "Maria, I [points to self]—want—you [points to child]—to listen [points to ear]." When the teacher has evidence that Maria understands each of these words so far, she continues, "Please, stand up [gestures with hands and then demonstrates]." Consequently, the teacher must pay attention to (a) delivery—for example, making sure to pronounce words clearly and using real objects and gestures; (b) content—making sure material is appropriate and familiar; and (c) environment—creating a comfortable atmosphere in which students have positive experiences that are relatively free of anxiety.

Systems of Language

When a person is learning English, he or she is learning not only the sounds of the language (phonology), how words are built (morphology), the meanings of the sounds (semantics), and the rules that govern the structure of the language (syntax), but also the particular situations in which these words would be used. The person also needs to know the social context—when and how to use it. Distinguishing when to use formal and informal expressions is as important as knowing grammatical rules and vocabulary words. One would not use the expression "Wazzup?" (what's up?) in addressing a priest or rabbi; however, it would be appropriate for saying hello to a friend passed on a city street.

Students will acquire the language systems by listening to and observing other people as well as receiving explanations. It is important to carefully plan lessons that involve students in activities with one another so they will have opportunities to develop purposeful expressions and increase their language ability. They will realize there is a difference in how one responds depending on whether it is a formal or informal interaction. The language they use with you, the teacher, will be different from the language they use in the cafeteria or on the playground.

Language Processes

There are four areas of language proficiency. The two related to oral performance are listening and speaking, with the component parts of pronunciation, grammar, and vocabulary. It is in these areas that students first develop mastery. There is ready stimulation and much social—not to mention survival—motivation to understand speech, to carry on a conversation, and to be able to ask questions. However, it must be noted that for most people who are learning a second language, there is a silent period that takes place. As students become accustomed to the sounds and meanings of sounds and symbols, they will be in a receptive rather than an initiating mode of behavior. They will speak little, if at all, in the beginning. Remember, this does not mean they are not learning; they are just processing what they hear.

The two areas related to written performance include the ability to read and write. The corresponding component parts are spelling, grammar, and vocabulary. As you have no doubt noticed, these areas take longer to develop. Students who lack proficiency in these areas have trouble in classes that focus on reading, such as history and literature courses. Given that it may take students up to 15,000 hours of exposure to learn a language, teachers must be very patient.

Content-Based Approach

Current research in language development calls for simultaneous development, fostering a whole language experience without fragmenting the systems into discrete parts. The current school of thought is to teach English using a content-based approach, that is, through subject areas rather than a focus on grammar. This is precisely the situation faced by the regular classroom teacher. As students are involved in meaningful learning activities that stimulate them on a cognitive level, they will develop the corresponding necessary English language skills. For example, as you introduce a unit on nutrition, the students will learn the terminology and expressions associated with food and health habits that contribute to daily life.

Achieving Competence

A student first develops simple conversational skills. Freeman and Freeman (1998) describe the results of the Cummins (1981, 1996) research in language acquisition. Conversational language, which Cummins referred to as developing basic interpersonal communicative skills (BICS) in a second language, takes one to two years. These skills of social communication are related to the settings in which they occur (school, neighborhood, store). They are characterized as contextual, in that the student gains meaning from clues in the situation—objects, pictures, gestures, and other aspects of nonverbal communication. Within two years, a student can participate in face-to-face conversation that is concrete and cognitively undemanding.

Often when verbal fluency is developed, people assume the student can perform equally well in reading and writing tasks. A Mexican teenager of my (Ellen) acquaintance moved to this country from Mexico City with his two older brothers. He attended high school for a while and then dropped out. I had been surprised by his academic difficulties, given that he was verbally expressive. When I asked him why he dropped out of school, he replied matter-of-factly that it was because he couldn't read the textbooks in English.

It takes five to seven years for a student to develop cognitive academic language proficiency (CALP), which requires literacy. This proficiency is characterized by the ability to understand academic language, which is often abstract, and the ability to function at an advanced cognitive level. Synthesizing information from different sources is an example of CALP.

Therefore, don't be surprised when children placed in regular classrooms are able to converse well and get along with their fellow students but have trouble mastering the content you present and so receive failing grades on tests. Their reading and writing skills may fall well below the level required for success. They may also lack the cultural experiences needed to achieve immediate success in the classroom and on standardized tests. As teachers, we need to develop activities in which all students can participate and demonstrate achievement. This chapter presents many ideas for your consideration.

Learning Rates

As with anything else about human behavior, there are vast individual differences in learning rates. Of the social and cultural factors that play a part, none should be taken in isolation.

- For some children, learning English will come easily and effortlessly. It is a goal they eagerly work toward. They will have support at home from their parents.

- For others, learning English may create serious problems as they are caught between two cultures that emphasize different values. Such students may feel torn between the demands of home versus those at school.

- Many students undergo extreme socioeconomic changes when they come to North America. As people move from rural to urban areas or from middle-class to lower-class status, the families face internal adjustment even before language becomes an issue. Regardless of status, culture shock is likely to exert some influence, especially during the first year.

- Some form of racial and ethnic discrimination is a reality of life for many students acquiring English. Many people who are already citizens here feel that new immigrants threaten the economic and social stability of our country. The impact of prejudice and discrimination leads to low self-esteem in students. They feel that less is expected of them, and this is often the case. Their perceptions of themselves will affect their school performance. As teachers, we need to be sensitive to and minimize such practices.

• Age makes a difference, too. Research has substantiated a phenomenon that most people have already observed: Children of certain ages can pick up another language faster than people at other ages. In fact, some studies show that children between the ages of 8 and 12 acquire a second language faster than children between the ages of 4 and 7 and those older than 12. Thus adolescents especially may be subjected to risky situations when they are placed in the regular classroom. They are expected to do grade-level academic work and are graded accordingly when they have not achieved proficiency in English. There is also great discussion on the appropriateness of requiring limited-English students to take standardized tests and high-stakes/proficiency tests when they are not fluent in English.

Proficiency Levels

Language development is usually divided into several levels of increasing complexity. School districts vary in the number of levels they use to determine the proficiency of students. In one sample district (Clark County, Nevada), the following stages are delineated:

1. Beginning Stage. At this level, very basic communication can be expected, with simple oral and written responses. Students may be hesitant to speak and tend to use a lot of nonverbal communication, such as pantomime, pointing to objects, and nodding the head to indicate "yes" or "no" in response to questions. Such individuals can show agreement or disagreement with "thumbs up" and "thumbs down" gestures. Another technique is to provide students with numbered sticks, then ask them a multiple-choice question and have them hold up the number that corresponds to their answer. Students can also draw pictures to demonstrate understanding and are comfortable matching words to pictures or objects.

At this beginning stage, teachers—and other students—need to do a lot of modeling for beginning students. Students will rely heavily on the teacher's body language, so gestures play a key role in developing understanding. It is important to use as many visual references as possible with pictures and artifacts. Providing opportunities for lessons that use art and music will be critical.

2. Early Production Stage. At the advanced beginning level, students add extended vocabulary and more complex grammar and focus on more complex reading and writing skills. Comprehension increases and students begin to speak. Students will be able to identify people and objects. They may understand the main idea of a presentation or a story but will not be able to understand each word or phrase. Students will be able to do short sentence-completion tasks. They will be able to repeat common expressions and begin to use common phrases on their own. There may be some mispronunciation as they begin to develop speaking skills, but there is no need to make corrections unless the meaning is unclear. Teachers can begin to ask simple yes-no, who, what, where, when, and why questions. The introduction of new vocabulary is important. "Think alouds" are helpful strategies for students. Rich learning environments that stimulate all the senses are needed.

3. Speech-Emergent Stage. At the beginning intermediate level, students begin to use descriptive terms in relating events. Pronunciation and intonation improve. Vocabulary increases. Students begin to initiate conversation. Comparison and contrasts can be accomplished, as students can handle academic concepts. Students are able to categorize and summarize information.

Teachers can ask open-ended questions and encourage students to respond. Support material continues to be important in the form of visual aids and graphic organizers. It continues to be important for teachers to model, reinforce, and emphasize student language.

4. Intermediate Fluency Stage. Student comprehension has improved considerably. At this stage students speak with few grammatical errors. They are able to share experiences, generate ideas, and give opinions. They begin to think in English rather than translate from their native language. Their language skills include debating, persuading, and negotiating with others. They can demonstrate higher-order thinking skills of synthesis, analysis, and evaluation.

Teachers need to provide opportunities for student interaction. Cooperative learning groups enable students to work on a task where speech is needed, but correct grammar is not crucial. Teachers can provide more complex academic work. Students can make use of print and online reference material to create projects. Teachers can introduce colloquialisms and idiomatic expressions. Providing opportunities to publish student work or give presentations will motivate students.

5. Fluency Stage. At this level students have near-perfect speech. They have no trouble interacting with native English speakers and read English with high levels of comprehension. Students may need help understanding abstract concepts. They continue to learn new vocabulary. Their reading and writing will be comparable to that of students their age who are native English speakers.

Teachers can expect students to give oral presentations, engage in role-play situations, and debate ideas. They can complete research projects with full reports. Support may be needed for abstract ideas. Providing sheltered English and cooperative learning strategies will continue to be important.

At the highest levels, students apply language skills to increasingly abstract thought as well as to highly technical material. Students continue vocabulary and grammar development as oral and written communication skills are further strengthened.

Determining Fluency Levels

Most school districts use a battery of standardized tests such as the CTB/McGraw-Hill Language Assessment Scales (LAS) developed by Sharon E. Duncan and Edward A. De Avila. The LAS Reading/Writing, for example, is available at three levels: Grades 2-3, Grades 4-6, and Grades 7-9+. The test items include vocabulary (synonyms and antonyms, language fluency, reading for information, mechanics, and usage) and ask students to do a writing sample. There are two forms available at each level for pre-post purposes, used with the LAS Oral to determine levels of listening, speaking, reading, and writing. The LAS were developed to measure English language proficiency and are used to classify and place limited-English students in classes. If your students have been assessed and you have access to their records, their scores will give you an indication of their skills.

A second test is the Idea Oral Language Proficiency Test, which also measures vocabulary, pronunciation, syntax, and functional use of language. Students are asked to distinguish between minimal pairs, identify objects, listen to a story, and answer questions.

Another common test is the Bilingual Syntax Measure, in which students are shown cartoon pictures and are asked to respond to pictures. This test measures whether students respond appropriately based on their grammatical expressions. It does not measure reading and writing ability. It is used to place students in classes.

A warning: The tests are often given when students first come to school, a time that can be overwhelming as they try to make sense of the new environment. Taking a placement test may create additional anxiety. The purpose of the test may not be clear; therefore, students may not understand the importance of the test. Also, the items on the test may not have any meaning for the students, so the scores may not give a true picture of students' capabilities. Use the information that is helpful, but remember that assessment needs to be an ongoing activity.

It is entirely possible that in one class of students, you may have limited-English speakers at different levels of proficiency, each with specific needs. Individualization of lessons is ideal but rarely practical. The next chapters address the needs of students at different levels and target resources for you to consider in working with students of different levels of proficiency.

High-Stakes Testing

One of the greatest challenges for children with limited English, even those who are fluent, is taking standardized tests. As states are adopting and implementing standards, they are incorporating assessments such as high-stakes testing. Olson (2001) reports that the American Educational Research Association and the National Research Council support the Standards for Educational and Psychological Testing conclusion that high-stakes tests, such as those for promotion or graduation, should not be based on a single test. Other information should be taken into account. However, what and how has not been established.

It is interesting to note that states are taking different approaches to high-stakes testing, such as proficiency tests linked with high school diplomas. Most districts are taking into account multiple measures, such as substitution of end-of-course exams. There is much variation from state to state. Olson (2001) describes the alternative New Jersey offers for its students. This state has a series of open-ended tasks that students do during the school year, called the Special Review Assessment. This assessment had been translated into eight languages at the time of this writing. Indiana offers an appeals process to students who fail, or as an alternative students may achieve a minimum grade point average in state-selected classes. Wisconsin, at present, allows districts to set the criteria for earning a diploma on the following: multiple measures, test scores, grades, and teacher discretion. Discussion on how to assess students will continue in the future.

First- to Second-Language Learning

Positive Transfer

Students will not be learning English independent of their first language. Some skills developed in the student's native language will transfer to English. For this reason, there is strong support for bilingual education, which allows students to continue cognitive development in their first language while learning English at the same time.

Positive transfer from one's native language to English takes many forms. Students who can read in one language know that the reason for reading is to acquire meaning. Students know that print is speech in written form. Limited-English-speaking students have already developed concepts in their native language and have given them names. These concepts do not have to be relearned in English; they merely need English labels. Such students have a foundation on which to build; they will look for the rules underlying the English language. Many will have developed the appropriate spatial orientation—reading from left to right and from top to bottom. Some will be familiar with the letters of the alphabet; others will have to be introduced to new symbols used in reading and writing. Reading comprehension skills—such as sequencing, inferring, and drawing conclusions—will transfer to English.

Cognates

There may be *cognates,* or words that are similar because they are derived from the same origin, that the student will be able to recognize in English. Words such as *color, radio,* and *terrible* are spelled alike in Spanish and English, although they are pronounced differently. Other words may have different spellings but will still be recognized, such as *excellent* (*excelente*) and *dentist* (*dentista*). The cognates quickly widen the student's vocabulary.

One student, who had previously been quite frustrated with her progress in learning English, had a major breakthrough when she recognized the number of English words that end in *tion.* She started rattling off a list of examples she had recently heard—sta*tion,* men*tion,* selec*tion,* func*tion*—giggling all the while. Finally, she recognized an underlying order to this "crazy language" when she was able to associate the ending with her native *cion,* as in *seleccion* or *funcion.*

Similarly, listening skills transfer from a first to a second language. Students will be sensitive to repetitious sounds and patterns in the language. They may need help with pronunciation and syntax, however, when they are ready to speak.

By pointing out the attributes of the student's first language that transfer to English, you can help the student feel less overwhelmed. This will also help him or her develop a positive attitude toward learning.

Negative Transfer

Students will also run into situations in which previous language learning will interfere with learning English. Teachers can make students aware of such instances of negative transfer. Common mistakes in pronunciation occur when students assume a letter in their native language makes the same sound in English. The *i* in English is pronounced as the word *eye* and not as the letter *e,* which is its sound in Spanish. Grammatical rules in the native language may not apply in English—such as the double negative. False cognates—words that appear to have similar meanings but don't—can cause students to make mistakes. *Assist* does not mean "to attend," as in Spanish, but "to help." With practice, the students will avoid these mistakes. Teachers can make lists of these words that might cause confusion for students.

Errors

Mistakes are to be expected. Unless the error interferes with communication, use the correct form in your response. It is more effective to rephrase and model the appropriate expression than to correct it. Research shows that emphasizing parts of speech and grammar drills is not an effective use of time. Even when students have mastered elements presented in formal instruction, they are not able to use them fluently in real communication situations inside or outside the classroom. Those who learned Spanish back in the 1960s and 1970s with the audiolingual method tell you today, "Pablo está bien pero Luisa tiene catarro." (Pablo is fine, but Luisa has a cold.) But no one has ever asked any of us how Pablo and Luisa are doing! Language cannot be isolated into bits and pieces. The best advice comes from a teacher who says, "Model, model, model. The more the students can actually see and hear what is expected of them, instead of just listen to instruction, is the best way to have students internalize what is being taught to them."

Code-Switching

At times, students will resort to using both their native language and English, sometimes in the same sentence. This is known as *code-switching.* Sometimes speakers will forget a word or will lack the necessary vocabulary. However, code-switching can be a conscious effort on the part of the speaker for expression in the most effective way (depending on the audience) rather than an inability to use either language correctly. There can be several reasons for using both languages, such as to emphasize a point or to show a personal connection. Scarcella (1990) remarks that code-switching can be a sign of advanced proficiency in both languages.

Language development is a gradual process. By setting reasonable expectations, utilizing positive transfer when possible, and assessing development throughout the year, you will lead your students down the path to becoming proficient communicators. Guidelines for structuring your personal means of communication, implementing practical teaching strategies, and making effective presentations follow in the next chapter.

The Silent Period

As we mentioned previously, students developing skills in English will often go through a silent period in which they will not initiate very much speech. During this time, children will be observing and listening to communication. They watch for body language and listen for intonation, pronunciation, and register (appropriate language for the situation). They observe social rules (how to begin and end a conversation, when to raise a hand). At the same time they are building up confidence and proficiency to speak. Some students may say very little except for routine phrases during this time.

The silent period can be very frustrating, especially for the teacher. This stage may last only a few weeks for younger children, but it may last longer for older children. You have no definitive way of knowing how much children understand, and this can be quite confusing. You will also have some students at the end of their silent period, whereas others will be in the beginning. You must have great patience in allowing the children to have the time they need to feel comfortable to speak. The more you work with students with limited English, the easier this will be.

Suggested Activities

1. Interview adults who were at one time limited-English students. Find out what their experiences were like trying to learn their new language. What did teachers do that was most and least helpful to them?

2. Tape-record a conversation between you and a student learning English. Evaluate your responses. Determine whether you are modeling correct expressions or giving mini-grammar lessons in response.

3. Make a list of the native languages of your students. Chart the similarities between the first languages and English.

4. Watch a foreign-language television station or movie. Describe how you try to figure out what is happening. List the supporting devices, such as dress, mannerisms, gestures, context, and other cues that help you figure out what might be going on. At which proficiency level are you operating?

Chapter Four

Strategies for Teaching

The review of second-language-related principles presented in the previous chapter offers a number of applications to the classroom. Although it has not usually been part of the training of teachers to learn specialized strategies for working with limited-English students, you will find that many of the experiences you have already been exposed to will lend themselves quite easily to adaptation to these situations. If you are hungry for practical things that you can do with children, the next chapters will stimulate your creativity not only in applying these methods but in adapting and inventing your own.

It's All About Motivation

Like so many other aspects of learning, motivation is often the key. Especially in the case of children with limited English, the challenge is not so much devising strategies for teaching but motivating students to learn the new language in the first place (Nunan, 1999). So although we include a cross-section of possible teaching strategies for working with this group of students, what you do is often less important than how you do it.

To refresh your memory, following are a number of things you can do to motivate those students who are particularly hard to reach (Burden, 2000):

1. *Make sure the difficulty of the work is matched to their ability levels.* If your assignments are too easy, students become bored and disengaged; if they are too difficult, students will become frustrated and tune out. It is between boredom and anxiety that "flow" states exist, where students are totally engaged, functioning at peak performance (Csikszentmihalyi, 1996).

2. *Provide useful structure.* Include clear expectations and realistic goals. Ensure that there are limited distractions. Plan for graduated steps toward success.

3. *Captivate student interest.* One of the most frequent complaints by all students is that what they are doing in class is not interesting or relevant to their lives. When limited-English students can see the clear connection between what is being taught and what they want (friends, opportunities, fun), they will be far more motivated to work.

4. *Provide support as needed.* Monitor progress carefully. Intervene before students give up or experience failure. Supply needed resources such as tutoring, peer help, and parent involvement.

5. *Show a lot of caring.* We mention this point a lot because it is so crucial. Encourage the students as much as you can. Reinforce their successes. Work on your relationships.

What to Say and How to Say It

Needless to say, when you are talking to someone who does not understand your language very well, it is important to speak slowly and distinctly. Don't distort your words or break them into syllables—just slow your rate of speech for beginners. Adjust your rate according to the proficiency of the students (Echevarria, Vogt, & Short, 2000).

Avoid the tendency that native English speakers have to speak louder than normal, as if the decibel level makes a difference in the other person's comprehension.

Talk about things present in the room, in the "here and now." Use props and pictures for reference. Accompany your speech with lots of gestures and actions to emphasize your meaning. Restate your message in several different ways. Ask the students questions about the points that you have made to check for comprehension. Make sure students have ample time to figure out what you have said. Extend your wait time after asking a question.

Frequent reinforcement is needed. After you present information, have students orally review the content in pairs. Then have them write a summary. This repetition in a variety of formats will help with comprehension and retention. Integrating topics around a theme is another way to provide students with multiple opportunities to work with a central body of language. Elementary teachers and teams in middle schools often use a thematic approach. Topics such as ancient civilizations or the rain forest make good thematic units.

Target Your Vocabulary

Teachers are always introducing new vocabulary and concepts. Identify which words will be central to your lesson. Present the vocabulary words first, and then use them with definitions in your learning activities. Use pictures to illustrate the words. Have students develop vocabulary cards or personal dictionaries and use drawings to represent the ideas. The authors of Project CRISS (Santa, Havens, & Maycumber, 1996) suggest using a "definition map" to help students determine categories, properties, and examples of words. By reviewing with students the qualities of a definition, this approach helps to personalize new words and integrate them into their working vocabulary. The map includes room for comparison items and illustrations. Use the same words and terms throughout your lessons.

Problem Areas

By becoming aware of your own speech, you will be more sensitive to those who do not speak English and can offer rephrasing or an explanation as needed, according to the puzzled looks of the students or their lack of appropriate responses. Idioms and abbreviations can be particularly frustrating.

Idioms. We use many idioms in everyday speech without being aware of them. Expressions such as "Cat got your tongue?" or "It's raining cats and dogs!" will leave students bewildered. One newly arrived student from Peru could not figure out what the word *pretty* meant: "I thought it meant, like beautiful, but you keep saying things like '*pretty* good.'" Trying to avoid idioms will have you "tripping over your tongue." Besides, if we cut out these rich expressions, we will narrow our range of expression and leave our speech dull and boring.

With beginners, it is wise to avoid idiomatic expressions. Simple, straightforward speech is preferred. With intermediate students, paraphrasing will be helpful. You can use such terms as part of lessons to acquaint your students with our "colorful language."

When students are confronted with an idiomatic expression, there are several strategies they can use to determine its meaning: (a) use context clues, (b) think about the literal meaning, and (c) use their background knowledge.

Acronyms. Often our speech is "peppered" with abbreviations. Remember to explain the meaning each time you use one, or refer to a poster that has the ones you use frequently. Also, you can develop a lesson on common acronyms. Do you use *PE, VIP,* and *ASAP* in your daily vocabulary? In education, we are especially enamored of these expressions (ELL, IEP, etc.) that are thoroughly confusing to the uninitiated. Have students develop a dictionary or vocabulary card file for reference.

Synonyms. Whenever appropriate, point out that different words can have the same meaning. Ask if students can think of examples in their native language to share with the class. This can lead to a general discussion on regional word usage as well. Do you *carry* people to the store (in the South) or *drive* them (in the North)? Is the engine of your car under the *hood* (United States) or the *bonnet* (England, Australia)?

Homonyms. Words that have the same pronunciation but different spellings and meanings challenge most elementary and secondary students. How do you distinguish *be* and *bee; sea* and *see;* or *two, too,* and *to*? How did you learn the difference between *principle* and *principal* or *capital* and *capitol*?

Homographs. Words that are spelled the same but have different pronunciations and meanings will make reading difficult for beginners. Both meanings will need to be presented before the student begins to use the vocabulary on his or her own. Contextual clues in the reading passage will aid the student's comprehension. Common examples include *lead, read, wind, tear.*

Noun Phrases. Expressions that consist of two nouns or an adjective and a noun and that combine ideas can be problematic. What is an *electrical engineer*? A train conductor who is plugged into an electric outlet? Consider a *mobile home park.* Does it change location? Students have difficulty understanding noun phrases in technical and scientific texts. These are especially difficult for Spanish speakers because of the word order.

Sheltered English

Freeman and Freeman (1998) point out that there are two different meanings for *sheltered instruction.* One refers to the composition of students; the other refers to delivery of content, such as math, social studies, science, and health. Some school districts use sheltered instruction as a way of grouping intermediate-proficient students in one classroom for a given subject. In that way, the children with limited English do not have to compete with the native speakers. Teachers modify the delivery of content to help students develop academically.

Teachers also use the technique called *sheltered English* with students in classes that contain both native and nonnative speakers. This relies heavily on the use of props, pictures, charts, and hands-on activities. Demonstrations and modeling are frequently used techniques. Teachers make sure students are able to understand what is being said by controlling vocabulary and idioms. This method involves using short, simple sentences with frequent paraphrasing and repeating. It involves all students in authentic activities, such as reading newspaper articles as part of a lesson in current events, using math manipulatives, reading a food chart, or engaging in a science experiment. It also acknowledges that students go through a silent period before voluntarily speaking. As mentioned earlier, it avoids error correction. Teachers also provide for small-group, cooperative experiences so that students have the opportunity to interact with their peers in meaningful communication as they accomplish academic tasks.

For example, in a lesson on baking a cake, you would want to have assembled all the ingredients you would need and all the utensils you would use. You might begin by showing an example of the desired end product to acquaint the students with the goal. Then, name each ingredient and let the students look, taste, and smell each item. Make sure the students can see what you do. Count out two eggs as the students watch. Describe your actions as you go along: "Now, I am cracking the eggs. Next, I will separate the white from the yolk." Present the steps of the recipe one at a time, as the students watch you model the desired behavior.

Likewise, in a science experiment, you would identify the equipment and chemicals you use by pointing to them individually and naming them: beaker, graduated cylinder, spatula, triple-beam balance. You would also describe your actions, such as measuring, pouring, stirring, observing, and recording. Indicate the states of being: solids, liquids, gases, and plasma.

Visual Aids

Objects, demonstrations, photographs, and pictures are vital to ensure comprehension. Students need concrete references, especially at the beginning levels of proficiency. Place vocabulary words with pictures on bulletin boards or display them with an overhead projector. Charts, graphs, and semantic webs will also serve the purpose of providing a visual reference.

Toys and tools that we take for granted might not be conventional items for the language-limited students. They may not have experienced snow, a garlic press, a pencil sharpener, or finger paint. It will be difficult for the students to find meaning in words related to objects or ideas with which they are not familiar. Careful preparation is needed to introduce background experiences for the students. Short video segments can be integrated before you teach a lesson. It also helps if you work toward creating an atmosphere and building relationships that make it safe and comfortable for students to admit they don't know what you mean. Consider recording a presentation or activity for playback at a later time. It can be used for reinforcement, review, or reteaching. A section on using technology is presented in the next chapter.

Provide Written Support

Vocabulary lists, with pictures if possible, and lists of expressions (such as *cracking the egg* in the previous example) will be helpful. Students with intermediate and advanced proficiency will benefit from outlines, graphic organizers, lecture notes, or summarized readings that coordinate with your lessons. Beginning students may need more structure; you might provide sentences with key words or terms left out that the student can fill in during your presentation.

Following is a review checklist of things to do in preparation for class:

1. Target the vocabulary and present it ahead of time. Identify and label the concepts you will cover so that students will be able to move from what they know to what they will need to know by the end of the lesson.

2. Pass out a reference guide, such as a desktop dictionary page, or post vocabulary words.

3. Provide students with an outline of your presentation.

4. Identify an appropriate graphic organizer, such as a Venn diagram or a sequence map.

5. Gather props, charts, and other visuals you will need.

6. Remember that conventional toys and tools that are familiar to you may require an introduction and hands-on experience time on the part of your students.

During class:

1. Focus on content and hands-on activities.

2. Avoid error correction.

3. Model correct responses.

4. Realize that students may be in a silent period.

5. Help students through problem areas such as idioms, homonyms, homographs, acronyms, and noun phrases.

6. Check for understanding.

7. Provide opportunities for nonverbal as well as verbal response to indicate that the students comprehend the new material or skill.

Learning Styles

Much of our discussion has been centered on generalizations about the way limited-English learners behave, what they need, or what works best. In fact, just as in every other facet of education, there are great individual differences that should be kept in mind. By paying attention to the variety of learning styles evident in the classroom, teachers can better individualize language development. Students will learn more easily and remember more when working in a style that best suits their ability, personality, and preferences.

Sensory Modality

The first set of learning styles includes those dominated by the senses, whether this includes vision, hearing, or touch. Some students learn best from seeing what is happening. They learn from text material, graphs, charts, pictures, and video. They learn through observation. Teachers who prepare advance organizers and use visual aids will help these students immensely.

Auditory learners prefer to hear new information. They are comfortable listening to a story or hearing a presentation. Teachers can help these students by recording information or providing audiotapes, videos, or CDs for review.

Tactile-kinesthetic learners like to move and touch things. Teachers can provide opportunities for manipulating objects, drawing pictures, and acting or role-playing situations. A multisensory approach will address all learners.

Global/Analytic Style

This learning style reflects the way people process information. Although most people use both sides of the brain simultaneously, they may have a distinct preference. The global learner uses the right hemisphere of the brain, focusing on spatial and relational processing. This student goes from whole to parts, looking for patterns and recognizing relationships. The analytic learner uses the left hemisphere for linear processing. This student goes from part to whole, looking for details on which to base an understanding. Some students vary their approach depending on the problem, whereas other students use only one way or the other.

Teachers need to model both approaches and provide opportunities for students to practice. For example, a history teacher can present the facts regarding the relative strengths and weaknesses of the North and South prior to the Civil War and ask students to generate conclusions or rank the causes. Later, he or she can present the topic of the Great Depression and have students identify examples.

Field-Independent/Field-Dependent Style

Students vary in the way they solve problems. Timm (1996) reports on the work of Herman Witkin, who explored how a person's perception is influenced by the environment by looking at how people perceive embedded figures from a surrounding field. Students who can differentiate objects from their backgrounds, or who are field independent, are able to work independently, are intrinsically motivated, and take an analytic approach to solving problems.

Those who are unable to separate items from their surroundings are field dependent and prefer to work with others, are extrinsically motivated, and take a global approach to solving problems. Students tend to prefer one style over the other. Timm's (1996) research shows that Hmong students tend to be highly field dependent, whereas other cultural groups lean more toward independence.

Teachers need to become aware of their teaching style. Do you prefer a controlled classroom where students sit in rows quietly doing assignments independently? Or do you structure a variety of paired and small-group activities where students work together on projects? Teachers need to provide activities related to both styles.

Field-independent students like to work alone. They thrive on competition and individual recognition. They work independently of the teacher and try things on their own. Teachers can serve these students by providing them with resources and watching them work on their own. Field-dependent students prefer cooperative learning activities. They like to help others and look to the teacher for explanations and directions. They like concepts that are related to them personally. Many children with limited English fall into the field-dependent style. Teachers can serve these students by working closely with them, having them work together in cooperative groups, and using material that is relevant to the student.

Jensen (1995) notes that learners who are field dependent prefer contextual cues. Field trips, experiments, and hands-on manipulatives support their learning. Field-independent learners do not need the "real thing" and are comfortable in libraries and classrooms looking at videos, books, or computers. The "bicognitive" students are comfortable in both situations.

Impulsive/Reflective

Some students are quick to guess solutions to problems or to answer questions. These students offer impulsive responses. At the other end of the continuum are reflective thinkers. They respond slowly to questions and take their time solving problems. These students do not want to make a mistake and carefully take their time to avoid errors. Teachers must provide ample wait time for these students and provide a supportive climate in the classroom for the reflective thinkers. The other students need to be encouraged to be patient as well. Reflectivity is a behavior practiced in many Far Eastern cultures, for example.

Although research has shown differences in cultural groups related to learning styles, it is dangerous to generalize. Each student should be recognized for his or her unique learning styles and level of proficiency.

Cooperation/Individualism

Another learning style relates to whether a student prefers to work alone or with others. Some students like to work by themselves independently and have their achievement noted. These children may enjoy competition. Teachers who make individual assignments will facilitate the learning environment for these students. Other students prefer to work collaboratively with others in small groups. In many cultures, cooperation among children is valued. Teachers who place students in pairs or small groups and structure cooperative learning activities will provide a classroom in which these students will be most comfortable. Of course, students should be given structured opportunities to engage in both situations.

Multiple Intelligences

In his research on intelligence, Howard Gardner (1983) originally created several categories: logical-mathematical, interpersonal, spatial, musical-rhythmic, intrapersonal, bodily-kinesthetic, verbal-linguistic, and naturalist. These different styles are also reflected in the ways that people manifest their creativity (Gardner, 1993). The following sections will briefly describe these intelligences and give examples of what teachers can do to help limited-English students in the classroom.

Logical-Mathematical

Students with logical-mathematical intelligence are able to solve mathematical problems and find numerical patterns. They are able to create reasons for solutions to problems using inductive and deductive thinking. They like order in the classroom and enjoy challenges. They like to categorize information, find sequences, and determine cause-and-effect relationships. They are skillful in predicting and analyzing. Teachers can foster this intelligence by using inquiry methods and project-based learning in the classroom that minimize essay writing and oral speech presentations that require fluency.

Interpersonal

Students with interpersonal intelligence are strong communicators. They will be leaders in the classroom with their ability to influence others. They work well with others in pairs and on teams. They work toward building consensus in group situations. Teachers can help foster this intelligence by structuring cooperative learning, learning centers, and service learning projects. Many English language learners will be more comfortable engaging in informal group settings rather than being in front of the whole class. This will also provide time for the teacher to interact individually with students.

Spatial-Visual

Students with spatial intelligence have a good sense of three-dimensional space. They rely on the sense of sight. They can judge people and items in relation to one another. They are attuned to what is in their environment, and they maneuver easily and find things easily. Teachers can provide rich classrooms for English language learners that include artifacts, pictures of objects, and maps. These students like to create art projects and build models that demonstrate what they know. They like to do skits and role plays.

Musical-Rhythmic

Students with musical-rhythmic intelligence can create patterns of sounds. They dance, clap, play instruments, and create music and songs, although singing well is not a feature. Teachers will find students very sensitive to sounds in the environments. They will find it useful to play different types of music to express ideas and set moods.

Students will enjoy songs, jingles, raps, and chants as a method of retaining information. Assignments can include putting information to music, creating musical performances, or doing projects that include music.

Intrapersonal

Students with intrapersonal intelligence think about how they think; they are highly reflective. They are aware of their own strengths and weaknesses. They need time to reflect and do self-assessments of their progress. They enjoy working by themselves. Teachers can provide private time for students to think and reflect on their interests, concerns, and their solutions to problems. Assignments can include essays, journals, guided imagery, and examining metacognitive skills.

Bodily-Kinesthetic

Students with bodily-kinesthetic intelligence are skilled in body movements and in manipulating objects. English language learners will benefit from using manipulatives and puppets in the classroom. They like to play charades, act out scenes, pantomime, and respond with gestures. They enjoy sports and games. Teachers can have students act out concepts, such as how the parts of a nerve process information or how a bill becomes a law. Assignments can offer options such as building projects with Legos, Popsicle sticks, or clay.

Verbal-Linguistic

Students with verbal-linguistic intelligence have good language ability and express themselves well. They like to debate and argue in the classroom. They like to read and discuss ideas. Teachers can provide supplementary reading for these students and give them opportunities for discussion in small groups. They also like to teach one another what they know. Teachers can provide opportunities for student research and presentation.

Naturalist

Students with naturalist intelligence understand the natural world. They can recognize and classify flora and fauna. They can discriminate various species. They are interested in animals and their behavior. They enjoy having plants in the environment. They are sensitive to changes in the weather and are fascinated by natural disasters and natural phenomena. Teachers can provide opportunities for students to come into contact with various animals. Science-related activities can include studying the weather and growing plants.

Teaching to Student Strengths

Different cultures emphasize particular kinds of intelligence. Jensen (1995) gives the example of tribes in Africa where all children are taught to sing and play music. Samoan and Fiji islanders are taught to be adept at celestial navigation. Although not all students will excel in every area, providing a variety of experiences in the classroom means that students will all have the opportunity to shine at one time or another. Likewise, students will have the opportunity to improve in their weaker areas.

Teachers should design multifaceted lessons that incorporate elements of all the intelligences over the course of a week. In this way, limited-English students, as well as all the children in the class, will have the opportunity to excel at one time or another. All students will have the opportunity to move out of their comfort range and into other areas. Likewise, assessments should be designed to contain elements of all the subgroups. Jensen (1995) suggests writing the topic or unit in the middle of a piece of paper and drawing spokes outward for each of the multiple intelligences. Then plan the activities and assessments you would use that relate to each area.

Using Multisensory Activities to Engage Students

Opening lines of communication with limited-English students can be difficult. Some children may nod their heads or say they understand because they think that behavior is what is expected of them. They imitate what they see the other children do. Some do not want to bring what they see as cultural disrespect on themselves, so they nod and smile. Activities such as drama, dance, and drawing can facilitate initial relationships in a nonthreatening environment that can be fun and stimulating at the same time. They also build on the multiple intelligences just mentioned.

Drama

Using drama in the classroom can help limited-English students with their communication skills in many ways. Students can respond to a prepared script that emphasizes pronunciation or a point of grammar, or they can write their own scripts or just improvise given roles. Acting offers a chance to use vocabulary and grammar and to practice enunciation in a meaningful way. A prop box is a must in the classroom. Acting also calls attention to body language—such as gesture, posture, and social distance—and to the paralinguistic features of language—such as pauses, intonation, and rhythm.

Having children role-play given social situations will be far less socially threatening than having them speak for themselves. It may provide a comfortable way for those students who do not initiate participation to be involved. If a mistake is made, it is the fault of the character, not the student. Students can use a cassette recorder to help them assess their speech. The students can practice by themselves before performing in front of the entire class. The teacher can supervise a rehearsal before the class performance to make sure the students understand the interpretation of the words and to give words of encouragement. Students who do not have roles in the plays will be prepared to follow and participate in discussion about the plays. Drama can be combined with writing and reading exercises.

For the very young or the very shy, try puppet shows or marionettes, in which the speech producer is not even seen!

Song and Dance

Singing can be a great change-of-pace activity. It can be used to energize or relax the students, depending on the selection you make. Just play a cassette tape or CD, and you are ready. Many teachers play classical music as background for their classes, because classical music may lower anxiety.

Auditory learners like listening activities. Music is highly connected to language: It processes sounds, conveys a message, and strikes an emotional response. Singing will help with pronunciation as well as with memory. Didn't you learn the alphabet with the alphabet song? "Head, Shoulders, Knees, and Toes" is a great way to teach parts of the body. Don't you know "In 1492, Columbus sailed the ocean blue?" Middle school students easily learn how a bill becomes a law by learning the lyrics with *America Rock,* a video by Scholastic Rock, Inc.

Singing will offer the students another means of expression. The lyrics can be used as a topic for discussion. Students can be encouraged to make up their own songs and present them to the class.

Sharing a little of American culture—whether through a square dance, a line dance, or the Hokey Pokey—is a great way to get all students up and moving and involved with one another. No language is necessary. Students mimic the leader's actions in time to the music. When they are ready, students can join in the words to the songs. For example, while doing the Hokey Pokey, elementary limited-English students will find themselves quickly learning the parts of the body. Meanwhile, in a history class, secondary students can be taught French court dancing of the Renaissance or the Charleston of the Roaring Twenties.

Another suggestion is to have the limited-English student teach everyone else a few of the dances that are popular in his or her culture. Requiring little in the way of verbal explanation, dance is taught primarily by demonstration.

Drawing

Students can record thoughts and feelings through pictures. They can draw their responses to questions or record observations. Students can develop a picture diary of activities carried out in the classroom, like the courtroom artist. All that is needed is paper and a box of crayons—or, for the more technologically sophisticated, a computer. For those who are uncomfortable with drawing, a selection of preprinted pictures or Colorforms might suffice. By asking questions that call for a visual response, you can learn a lot about your students—who the members of their family are, what they like to eat, where they like to go. Their interests, interpretations, and understandings of the world around them will be reflected in their artwork. Drawings can later be labeled as language skills progress. Pictures can enhance vocabulary development. Drawing can be used for small-group projects. Two to four students might be assigned the task of doing a poster or chart related to a topic of study. For example, students of any age and ability could design a travel brochure after completing a geography unit.

You can check students' abilities to follow directions by asking them to perform a set of instructions using pictures. For example, direct the students to put a circle around one item and make a square around another. Or have them move their pencils two blocks east, then two blocks south, to check comprehension of geographic directions. A middle school teacher explains:

I have them do a lot of drawing. As they become more comfortable with the drawing I have them start adding words of English that they have learned and to use them whenever possible. I continue this throughout the year and they are soon to the point of using mostly English. I have seen the results this year, as I'm teaching an 8th grade science class this year, and most are the kids I had in my classes last year in history.

Drawing can be a useful assessment tool, too. At the elementary level, students can draw the effects of a science experiment, and at the middle school level, students can illustrate stories they have read. At the high school level, you can provide pictures related to a historical event and have students sequence them to check the understanding of cause-and-effect relationships.

Building Literacy

The language experience approach (Nurss & Hough, 1992) is an example of a student-centered technique that ensures the development of relevant materials appropriate for the learners. Students create their own reading material after discussion of a topic in which key words are recorded. They determine the purpose, the form, and the audience for their writing. The teacher or aide writes down the words of the students exactly as they are dictated, and the students copy the text. As students become more capable, they will take on the initial writing, too. Correction is held off until the selection is re-read and questions arise. As students reread the selections, they develop their reading ability.

This whole language approach has been found effective with students of all ages. The approach allows students to build on past experiences and incorporate new information with what they know. Research shows that effective language development takes place when the classroom provides opportunities for students to generate, read, and respond to their own writing.

The writing can then be published or taped for others. Publication of student work not only provides motivation but also validates their work. It provides low-stress support for students learning a new language (Herrell, 2000). This activity can be used in conjunction with any content area and at any grade level.

Writing

Cary (2000) reminds us that the key to improving writing is to have students identify real-world purposes for their efforts. This means building on student interest and emphasizing the process rather than the product alone.

Journals

The development of writing skills can be promoted through the use of dialogue or communication journals in which the student and teacher write to each other (Nurss & Hough, 1992). In this interactive process, the teacher responds to the student's entries or asks questions. The teacher does not correct the student's writing but may incorporate a correct form of expression in the responses. Prompt feedback is required for this activity to be successful.

There are many benefits to this activity. Students get personal attention from the teacher. The journals provide a way for the students and the teacher to get to know each other. They are both actively engaged in communication. Also, the students can ask questions that they may not be comfortable asking aloud.

Letter Writing

Writing letters is an excellent way to build language skills in a meaningful way. It is a manageable task that has an authentic audience. Many teachers use writing to pen pals as a regular activity. Students can write to each other or to another class. Those with computer access can send electronic mail messages and can expect quick returns.

Publishing

Selecting topics of student interest will also help encourage students to work on their writing skills. Beginners will need lots of support. Providing the format, vocabulary word boxes, outlines, and graphic organizers may be appropriate, depending on your students. Students like to have their work read. Publishing their writing in a newsletter or a booklet will motivate your writers. Advanced writers will need help as well. A variety of writing assignments—from book reports to poetry to research papers—will need a full introduction for those who have not been previously exposed to these types of writing assignments. Teachers will need to show examples and explain the requirements of each project.

Reading

The selection of reading material needs careful consideration. Students need reading that is just above their level of understanding and that is interesting. Choosing culturally relevant material will make a big difference. If students read about their culture, they will begin to make connections and build upon their prior experience. Having selections about people who are similar to them validates their experiences. You will need books at all different levels to meet your students' changing needs. Teachers have found that providing many books on one topic enables students to come into contact with the same vocabulary and grammar. What they read in one book will be reinforced in succeeding books. This is called *narrow reading*. If you can provide books in the native language as well, the concepts are sure to be clear to the students. Science and history classrooms, in particular, should have many resources available to students for research.

Objectives

Nurss and Hough (1992) point out that content area teachers will need to teach reading comprehension skills. Santa et al. (1996) state that one of the most critical steps to reading comprehension is to set the purpose for reading. Some textbooks have a list of objectives or guiding questions at the beginning of each chapter or section indicating what the student will learn. For other types of reading, the teacher will need to model and discuss the reason directly with students to identify why they are being asked to read a story, an article from a magazine, a historical diary entry, a graph, or a newspaper article. For example, they will be reading to gather information, to identify the cause and effects of a particular event, or to identify the author's point of view.

Resources

With any reading task, students should have access to bilingual dictionaries. However, if you see a student using the dictionary frequently, then you can assume the level of the text is too difficult and try to find something simpler.

Students should have easy access to libraries. Note that some children will be unfamiliar with libraries and will need not only an introduction but also an orientation to the library collections and how to access them. As some children do not have time to read at home or are not accustomed to reading at home, time in class should be provided. Parents will need to be informed that students are allowed to keep the books for a set period of time and then must return them promptly, as opposed to assigned textbooks, which they keep for the semester or school year. The more students read, the better readers they will become.

Support

Getting students to read is very challenging. The first step is to activate or build on prior knowledge. The students need to relate what they are going to read to something familiar or something previously studied. Begin by presenting a topic, for example, an election, or an experience, for example, loneliness, that students will recognize. Preparing written and visual support, as mentioned earlier, will be helpful. If possible, provide summaries in the students' native language.

Some teachers like to begin with a simulated experience. For example, when studying industrialization, history teachers have students simulate what it is like to work on an assembly line. Students are divided into groups, and then each group is given a task, for example, measuring, cutting, assembling, and stapling paper for notepads. Economics teachers simulate the marketplace by passing out paper bags filled with odds and ends and allowing students to trade with one another.

Integrated Strategies

A successful integrated reading strategy is the KWL (Ogle, 1989), in which the teacher begins by identifying what students already *know* (K) about a topic, what they *want* to learn or know more about (W), and then later, when they have finished the unit of study, what they have *learned* (L). This exercise begins by activating students' prior knowledge and serves to review needed vocabulary for the limited-English student. You can also teach new concepts at this time that will be useful in understanding new material.

A second common integrated strategy is SQ3R. Students first *survey* (S) the passage to be read, and then they create *questions* (Q) from headings and words in bold print or read the questions found at the end of the section before they *read* (R) the passage. After reading they *recite* (R) by creating an oral or written summary of what they have read. Finally, they *review* (R) by answering the questions they created for the passage.

Another technique is Multipass (Deschler, 1983), where students preview information before active reading. To implement this technique, first ask students to read just the headings and subheadings in a passage and develop questions. Then direct students to go through the passage a second time to look at the visuals and read the captions. Next, have students read sentences that have boldfaced words and use the context to determine the meaning of the words. Finally, have students read the introduction and conclusion. Only after students have made these four "passes" through the reading assignment are they directed to the actual reading.

Reading Challenges

Reading literature will be the greatest challenge. A story with many subplots will be difficult for students to follow. Poetic imagery will be difficult for them to understand. Overwhelming detail will be frustrating for them. Drawing inferences can be a challenge. Therefore, careful preparation is a must. By anticipating these problem areas and addressing them before the actual reading, teachers will structure successful experiences.

Difficult passages will merit classroom discussion using reading strategies such as the "think aloud." As you read a selection, you describe your own thinking process and express your thoughts out loud. In other words, you identify the specific strategies you use as you read. For example, you show students how you sort through the text for the main ideas, try to figure out the meaning of a word from its context, and reread passages that you say are unclear after the first reading. You verbalize the questions you ask yourself as you read, such as "What is this author trying to say?" when you don't understand a passage or "I think there is going to be conflict" as you predict the ending.

Current instructional approaches have teachers model the process and then engage students in the think-aloud process and work together to construct meaning. This focuses student attention and forces students to take their time thinking about what they are reading.

Processing

Note-taking strategies can be taught to students to assist them with comprehension, such as two-column note taking (main idea/detail notes). Note taking done during reading will help focus student attention on the material.

Postreading activities are just as essential to help students organize their learning and remember what they have read. Depending on the subject, graphic organizers such as sequence mapping, character mapping, concept mapping, Venn diagrams, process notes, or problem-solution graphic organizers may be appropriate as well as completion of the KWL and SQ3R strategies described previously and note taking. These strategies help students transform the information to become their own. They work with the material by summarizing, categorizing, and giving examples, all of which give them an opportunity to review the material after they have read it. This goal can also be met by having students share, discuss, and present to each other in pairs (Think-Pair-Share; Kagan, 1994), to small groups, or to the whole class.

Speaking

As we have discussed, students will speak when they are ready. We review other important points to remember. First, establish a comfortable, safe environment, one in which the students feel accepted and worthy. Provide a meaningful situation in which students will be motivated to participate, such as when they serve as the expert in a subject. This can be facilitated by taking their interests into account. Do allow students some opportunities to speak in their languages of choice, even if their choice isn't English. By providing them with a voice in the classroom, at least with each other, they will feel more comfortable. Cary (2000) reminds us to reduce the amount of teacher talk so that student speech will increase. As mentioned before, it is important to restructure questions—from closed questions requiring one-word answers to open-ended questions—so that students will respond according to their level of fluency.

Small-group activities provide students with the opportunity for social interaction. Freeman and Freeman (1998) note the following with respect to group work. Students enjoy working in groups; they find it motivating. The amount of language increases, as does the quality of the language. There are all sorts of choices for the teacher, from structuring simulations to literature circles, collaborative learning projects, and cross-age tutoring.

A Community of Learners

In order to maximize learning in the classroom and to encourage students to speak their new language skills, they must be actively involved. The most effective way to make this process occur is to develop a community of learners.

Thomas and Collier (1997) find that students will benefit most in classrooms that are student centered, with the teacher in the role of facilitator. Examine your objectives to determine how you can provide opportunities for students to practice, apply, and evaluate the ideas you have presented. Then go on to see how you can help students to structure their own learning. As students interact with each other, they will learn both content and language.

Cooperative Groups

In general, cooperative learning involves students working together in small groups in which they are responsible for their own learning as well as that of their teammates. The nature of the task varies according to the particular technique implemented. Using David and Roger Johnson's learning-together method (1998), students work together to produce a group project. Students following Robert Slavin's methods (1988) are placed in student teams to help each other learn material. Slavin's groups are based on team recognition, individual accountability, and an equal opportunity for success.

Yael and Shlomo Sharan's group investigation method (1992) features a constructivist approach to learning in which students work together to identify problems, plan how to study them, collect information, and present reports in interesting and creative ways. Language-limited students benefit in many ways from cooperative learning activities. As noted previously, cooperative learning groups may be more culturally consistent for some students than whole-class learning is. Students receive practice with language as well as practice with content. The teacher can carefully structure the composition of groups to combine students who have strong language and academic skills with those learning English as a second language.

The first activities can be designed to build communication patterns and trust, beginning with nonverbal activities that require each member to participate in order for the task to be successfully completed. This might include putting a puzzle together when each member has a piece or certain "trust" activities in which children work together as a cohesive team.

If there is more than one limited-English speaker in the class, they can be grouped together for support or separated for greater exposure, depending on their needs and your intentions. All students will need to be taught the communication and social skills needed to work in a group and the various roles that group members will take. All students can be taught how to give help and how to explain solutions to problems rather than just supplying answers to questions.

Discussion of the group process should follow the cooperative learning experiences to ensure that group responsibilities (recorder, time captain, encourager, spokesperson, etc.) are divided and that each member has an opportunity to contribute to the group discussion or task. Cooperative groups give the limited-English speaker a nonthreatening situation in which to rehearse responses that will later be called for in front of the entire class. It also will provide them with peer models. Changing group membership after a period of time will increase the number of people with whom students interact.

Cooperative learning groups, as with all the methods suggested in this chapter, require you to consider the inner world of your limited-English students—what it is like for them to be strangers in a strange land. Your job, as much as possible, is to help them to feel welcome. Through the strategies included in this chapter, and many others of your own invention, you are demonstrating how responsive you can be to their needs.

Suggested Activities

1. Interview teachers who work with limited-English students and find out about their most effective strategies and tips for working with this population.

2. In small groups, talk to one another about your own dominant intelligence or creativity style and how you have learned best throughout your life.

3. During the discussion in the previous activity, keep track of all the idioms and expressions you use that might not be immediately comprehensible to nonnative English speakers.

4. Brainstorm a list of activities and strategies that you intend to use when working with limited-English students. Include some that you invented yourself.

Chapter Five

Teaching Strategies Borrowed From Language Instruction

Whereas the previous chapter offered tips and strategies of a general nature that can be used in a variety of classroom settings, there are also a number of methods that can be borrowed from the work of foreign and English language teachers. These can be adapted in a number of different ways, depending on your grade level, subject area, teaching style, and particular student needs.

What We Can Learn
From Foreign Language Instruction

The work of foreign language teachers offers a variety of techniques that can be applied in the regular classroom to help you work effectively with all your students. Listed here are brief descriptions of some of the more useful approaches, with examples of how to apply them. Some will be appropriate for use with the entire class; others will be more suitable for small groups or individuals.

Direct Method

In the 1920s, the direct method of teaching foreign language became popular in the United States as an alternative to the previous century's reliance on grammar translation techniques to teach classical languages. Speech, with an interest in proper pronunciation rather than writing, was the goal. Teachers of the direct method speak only the language to be learned in class. Lessons are sequenced in progression of complexity. The receptive skills of listening and reading are taught before the productive skills of speaking and writing. Attention is given to the age and background of the student and to relating the language to its culture.

The direct method emphasizes the fact that age and background have a bearing on language learning ability. It is important to use vocabulary suitable for the age of one's students. Knowing the background of your students, as noted in Chapter 1, will help you choose lessons that are motivating and stimulating to them as you teach English through a content area. In teaching the steps of the scientific method, for example, let the students suggest a hypothesis to test, a question they propose, or something they want to know more about.

Today's classroom teachers can benefit from this method by seeing how the use of English is a part of our culture. Even the words are determined, to a great extent, by the cultural constructions of our world. For example, a classroom exercise in a social studies class might ask students to compare (with explanation for limited-English students) slang words used today versus those used during the 1920s. Ask your students what the modern counterparts are for such terms as *giggle water, big cheese, bees' knees, cat's meow,* and *spiffy.*

The Natural Approach

Communication activities in a low-anxiety setting are central to Krashen's (1996) natural approach, which was developed in collaboration with Tracy Terrell. This method is especially effective for beginning and younger English students. The teacher models speech using high-interest, high-context topics to present vocabulary in a controlled manner. For example, the teacher might do an introduction activity at the beginning of the school year by describing the people in the room and asking questions about them.

The teacher guides the students in conversation through four stages. In the first stage, students communicate with nonverbal behaviors—movement and gestures. ("If you have brown eyes, stand up.") In the second stage, students respond to closed questions with one or two words. ("Are your eyes brown or blue?") In the third stage, students speak in phrases or complete sentences. ("I have brown eyes.") In the last stage, students can carry on conversations with minor guidance. ("I know a boy who has beautiful brown eyes and . . .".) The teacher gradually adds new vocabulary as the students slowly progress. Students respond at their own pace and are encouraged to realize they don't have to understand every word. The teacher does not correct errors, so anxiety levels are not raised. After the students have developed intermediate oral proficiency skills, reading and writing are added.

An important contribution of this method is the identification of the stages of speech emergence. Teachers can structure their questions according to the ability levels of their students. Those who have very limited proficiency, in the preproduction stage, can be asked to use gestures to indicate a response or circle pictures on a page that represent ideas. Those with low proficiency, in early production stages, should be given yes-no questions or multiple-choice questions in which the answer is supplied. Also effective are sentence-completion exercises or questions that require one- or two-word answers.

When students reach the fourth stage, teachers can ask for information, explanations, and interpretations or give problems for students to solve. As with other strategies mentioned, you do not correct the students' mistakes. The goal is communication.

From the natural approach, the regular classroom teacher once again realizes that students will have to be exposed to a great deal of language before they respond verbally and that they proceed through a series of stages. Activities need to be structured to keep the anxiety level low for students with material that will not overwhelm them.

Total Physical Response

The Total Physical Response (TPR) technique, developed by James Asher (Bowen, Madsen, & Hilferty, 1985), begins by incorporating listening skills with movement. Asher noted that mothers often talk to their children using the imperative, for example, "Turn around" or "Give me the ball." Used primarily with beginners, this approach couples commands with action. The teacher begins by modeling simply stated directions using controlled vocabulary to build language, and students respond with the appropriate action: "Stand!" "Sit!" Then the teacher expands to complete sentences: "Walk to the door." "Open the door." Listening is emphasized, and the students are not pressured to speak. Seely and Romijn (1995) have extended TPR to involve students in more complex dialogues and role-play situations.

In the regular classroom, the teacher will find that new students with beginning English skills will respond well to commands used frequently that relate to classroom routines. Identify the requests you frequently make, such as "Clear your desks," "Take out a pencil," and "Line up at the door." You can call on an individual to demonstrate that the commands are understood. Students are not required to give a verbal response.

Suggestopedia or Suggestology

Georgi Lozanov's (1979) method concentrates on providing a warm, relaxed, pleasant environment. Paying close attention to the student's emotional state, the teacher's approach is to create receptive students. Relaxation techniques and breathing exercises are used to begin each session to enable students to tap their latent ability to learn a language.

Suggestopedia requires an informal setting such as a living room. Musical interludes are also used for relaxation. The students are given an identity to assume, complete with a distinct personality and profession. The lesson then proceeds over the next several days. First, the teacher introduces lines of dialogue with scripts and gives an informal explanation. Next, the teacher presents the dialogue with three different intonations (normal, soft, strong). Finally, the dialogue is read expressively set against music. Listening and speaking are emphasized over reading and writing.

Although the format of the Suggestopedia lessons may not be practical and the informal setting not available in public schools, the regular classroom teacher may find that providing an anxiety-free atmosphere is a good guideline to follow. Creating an attractive and inviting room will set the mood for students of any proficiency. If there are too many objects or pictures, students may easily be distracted by overstimulation. Color, lighting, and temperature, as well as the size of seats, will affect students' behavior. It is important to make sure the students' physical and emotional needs are being met.

Music can be used as an agent for relaxation and change of pace in the classroom to set an affective tone. Students may enjoy having music in the background while they are working individually or in small groups. Another application of this method would be to vary poetry readings or sections from literature according to the pattern suggested by this technique.

Counseling-Learning or Community Language Learning

Introduced by Charles Curan (1976), the counseling-learning or community language learning approach focuses on the relationships between the people involved. The teacher's role is to understand the needs and feelings of the students learning a language and to help them reach their goal by establishing trust and cooperation in the group. The teacher, who must be bilingual, is known as a *knower* or *counselor-teacher.* At first, the students sit in a circle and are invited to talk to one another in their native language. The teacher is located outside the circle and translates the students' conversations. The students repeat the translations. The statements are taped and played at the end of the lesson as review or as a subject for a grammar lesson.

Students progress through five stages as they gain confidence, increase their ability to speak to and understand one another, and become less dependent on the teacher. As the students become more competent, the teacher becomes more active in asking questions, making corrections, and adding explanations. Finally, the teacher indicates by cue that students are making mistakes or that more appropriate expressions could be used. The students like the control they have over their learning and the group process that fosters cohesion and respect for one another.

The role of the teacher in this approach is that of a consultant. No longer viewed as an authority whose task is to criticize, the teacher's job is to help students feel comfortable and to minimize anxiety. A safe environment is created in which students can explore their feelings, beliefs, and experiences. Attention is placed on group process, and students are encouraged to talk about what is meaningful to them. The teacher guides the students in their discussions. The classroom becomes student centered. Children's needs for social interaction are acknowledged and met.

In the regular classroom, the teacher will find it helpful to create a seating arrangement that facilitates communication. If possible, arrange the furniture in your room so students can sit in circles to talk to one another. In this way, a student-centered, nonthreatening classroom environment is created. When students sit in rows or at opposite ends of tables, it is difficult for them to interact with one another.

Applying Strategies
Used by English Language Teachers

Besides approaches to foreign language learning, we can use models that have been developed by English language teachers as a separate discipline. We will examine how regular classroom teachers can adapt strategies from the Cognitive Academic Language Learning Approach (CALLA) and then Principles for Success. Finally, we look at the Joyful Fluency Model, which incorporates principles from brain research into the development of language.

Cognitive Academic Language Learning Approach

Chamot and O'Malley (1989) developed a program especially designed for the intermediate English language learner. CALLA is targeted for students who have developed social communication but are not ready for grade-level academic work. For example, these students need help transferring concepts from their native language to English. In the CALLA classroom, the teacher identifies and presents not only academic language skills but also specific academic content and corresponding learning strategies. With respect to content, the CALLA teacher would focus on science first because of the nature of the hands-on experiments involved in the study of the discipline. Next, mathematics is introduced with manipulatives for concrete experiences. Then social studies is presented, followed by language arts. The last two areas are more challenging because of the abstract nature and cultural references that may be foreign to the students. High-level thinking skills are introduced as appropriate to the age of the students.

The teacher also introduces, explains, and models learning strategies. Chamot and O'Malley (1989) group the learning strategies into three categories: metacognitive strategies, which monitor comprehension; cognitive strategies, in which students interact with the content material; and social-affective strategies, where students interact with others to help learn material and demonstrate a positive attitude. Students practice until they become proficient. With this background, students are carefully prepared to enter mainstream classes.

There are five phases in the CALLA lesson. In each phase the teacher identifies the specific content and appropriate learning strategies. The teacher prepares the students by introducing new vocabulary and then activating learning strategies such as elaboration (evoking prior knowledge, providing advance organizers), previewing what's to come, and selective attention (pointing out key vocabulary and concepts). During the presentation of material, the teacher presents the new information or skill with direct instruction and then by means of the learning strategies such as elaboration, note taking, checking for comprehension, inferring, and imagery. The third phase involves structured practice.

Preferably, the students will be involved in an application of a hands-on activity, either individually or in groups. Students apply learning strategies such as planning for a task, using resources, summarizing information, creating a graphic organizer, or asking questions for clarification. Phase 4 is the evaluation stage, in which both students and the teacher assess what was learned in terms of the identified objectives. The last phase is for expansion, where students will continue to use what they have learned or apply what they have learned to a new situation.

In the regular classroom, teachers can use many of these elements, such as previewing lessons and reading assignments, demonstrating how to use a textbook, and creating a KWL chart. Teaching vocabulary will help students selectively attend to their reading. Reminding students of cognates, providing contextual clues, and grouping words together are strategic aids. Teaching before-, during-, and after-reading strategies is a must in any content area. All students need help with their listening skills.

As an example, students practice taking notes in a "T list" format as described here:

1. Main ideas are written on one side of a paper and supporting details on the other side.

2. Students practice speaking based on the notes they have made, usually with a partner to minimize performance anxiety.

3. During the sharing, each student takes notes on what the other student is talking about, again listing the main ideas.

4. Students next develop test-taking skills by reviewing the format of tests, the process of "bubbling" responses on a Scantron form, and strategies for selecting answers to multiple-choice questions.

Structured exercises such as this one help students to develop sound habits for listening to, retaining, and organizing new material.

Principles for Success

Freeman and Freeman (1998) developed a set of guidelines for teachers who work with students who do not speak English well. Their principles for success include the following:

1. Design curriculum around themes. Based on the concept that learning proceeds from whole to part, students need to see the whole picture, the big idea, before concentrating on the details. For example, when learning to speak, children use phrases to represent whole ideas, such as *more* for "I would like some more" or *cookie* for "I want a cookie." With early spelling, children use letters, often consonants, to represent words, leaving out vowels or silent letters. With respect to reading, the idea of whole-to-part is supported by setting the purpose for reading, as presented previously.

Thematic units can be based on significant questions. This enables limited-English learners to see the whole picture and make connections to their own lives and experiences. Then they can explore details and find specific examples. Change, cooperation, conflict, and movement—these are concepts that all students can relate to. The vocabulary will be reinforced as it is used in multiple situations and can be adjusted according to the ability of the students.

2. Create learner-centered activities that build on students' interests and actively involve them in the learning process. Establishing writing workshops is a way to foster a student-centered classroom. From books and newsletters to Web sites, students can explore the answers to what McTighe and Wiggins (1998) refer to as "Essential Questions" and publish their results. Think of the essential questions as umbrellas under which smaller, more precise questions fit. Build units of study around these smaller questions, or divide the unit of study and have small groups research and present sections to the whole class. The objective is to excite students about finding the answers to the questions so that they will be motivated and engaged in learning activities.

3. Select lessons that will have meaning for the students and engage them directly. The purpose of each lesson must be clear to students for them to use their energy to get involved. The regular classroom teacher can use authentic reading and writing activities and choose relevant themes and topics.

4. Involve students in social interaction. Students negotiate meaning with one another and therefore need opportunities to work together in pairs and small groups. The regular classroom teacher can structure small-group cooperative learning tasks. Limited-English students will have the opportunity to express their ideas, check their understanding, ask questions for clarification, and improve their conversation skills. Active student participation increases when students work in groups. The classroom teacher then has time to circulate and give individual attention to the students.

To be successful, the following factors need to be addressed: organization of resources, clear directions, announced time limits, and time to report back to the class. Social studies teachers can use simulation activities to provide social interaction embedded in the mastery of content. Interact, a company that produces classroom simulation activities, has a range of topics at different levels related to U.S. history and world history. Teachers Curriculum Institute's History Alive! Program for U.S. and world history also has excellent materials. English or language arts teachers can use pen pal letters and literature circles as the purpose for social interaction. Cross-age tutoring is another program consideration when working with students from different grade levels. Social action and active citizenship projects are another way for teachers to get students involved in their community, identify problems, research solutions, and select the best one for implementation. We the People . . . Project Citizen has student guides available in English and Spanish.

5. Develop lessons that develop oral and written language skills simultaneously. Limited-English students need to be introduced to reading and writing from the beginning. Even beginning students need exposure to both speech and print. Naming and labeling are the first step. Art, music, and drama activities will help students develop a foundation on which communication skills can grow.

6. Recognize the students' first languages and cultures. Current research (Thomas & Collier, 1997) shows that bilingual education is often the most effective delivery system. Not only do students who have been in a bilingual setting do better academically, but they show higher self-confidence and a more positive attitude toward school. Students learn concepts best in their first language and are able to stay on track to graduation. They learn the academic content and critical thinking skills needed to be successful. In the best of circumstances, they transfer these skills to English as they gain more experience and practice. As noted earlier, when students feel that their culture is valued and that they have contributions to make, they feel better about themselves and their roles as students in school.

7. Show full faith in the potential of the learner. Maintaining a positive attitude and appreciating the contributions of each child will show your support. Many English learners will identify the one teacher who made a difference in their lives by taking the time to show interest and encourage them. Express confidence in their ability. Acknowledge their progress. Be positive and enthusiastic.

Brain-Compatible Second-Language Acquisition

As Dhority and Jensen (1998) explain, creating a joyful environment will facilitate language learning. The teacher's goal is thus to facilitate an atmosphere in class that makes learning fun and exciting. Their Joyful Fluency Model incorporates the following brain-compatible principals:

1. Language learning involves the whole brain. Both hemispheres are active in the process.

2. The brain looks for meaning. Learning lists of vocabulary makes little sense. Using words in a relevant context that has personal meaning for students does make sense.

3. The brain works best in settings that are moderately challenging and that provide high levels of feedback. Although students need a lot of feedback on their speech, it does not need to come solely from the teacher. Peer interaction is desirable.

4. High stress or threat creates anxiety, which is counterproductive. Low stress is preferable, in that it causes individuals to be attentive. Arrange the furniture in your room so it will be comfortable. Set realistic expectations and deadlines. Stay away from sarcasm and anything that would embarrass students.

5. The brain thrives on processing a constant stream of audio, visual, and tactile information. Students need a stimulating environment.

6. Much of what we learn is acquired rather than "studied." Students need multisensory experiences in which student involvement and interaction with others are key elements.

7. Emotions influence student learning. Whereas negative emotions can turn students off, positive emotions will spur students on.

8. The brain creates learning pathways, rather than "memories." All learning can be retrieved if the right pathways are stimulated. Short, student-meaningful, event-oriented situations are compatible with the way the brain learns. Kinesthetic, multisensory experiences are most conducive to this goal. The brain needs time to process new information. Short periods of reflection are key to retention.

9. Learning is a total-body experience. The brain is sensitive to light, smell, touch, sound, and movement. It is easier to remember experiences that involve different parts of the body. The physiological state of the body affects how the individual learns.

10. The brain has developed to specialize in communication. We are social beings. Students should be given multiple opportunities to talk to one another in role plays, debates, discussions, brainstorming sessions, and cooperative group activities.

11. The brain uses language as a form of communication instinctively. Although teachers can aid in the process, students acquire language from exposure to it, rather than direct instruction.

The Joyful Fluency model emphasizes the role of the teacher as a facilitator rather than an instructor. He or she is responsible for creating a positive, caring atmosphere in the classroom; fostering constructive attitudes; showing concern and appreciation for each student; and encouraging students to work together.

The teacher structures the learning for all students who work individually and in groups in a multisensory environment that is pleasant and comfortable for students. Physical factors to consider are lighting, temperature, furniture arrangement, background music, and peripheral stimuli. Natural lighting, living plants, ventilated rooms, and chairs and tables that can be easily rearranged are recommended. There should be ready access to easels, flip charts, or white boards. Visuals can be posted on bulletin boards.

The final consideration is that of selecting materials that will be appropriate for students—not too easy, not too hard. Organize supplies so that they are readily accessible. Look for handouts and graphic organizers that are easy to read and colorful if possible. Use multimedia presentations, demonstration, and simulations. Computers are a powerful technology for limited-English learners. Videotapes, audiotapes, posters, maps, puppets, costumes, and props all fall under the category of materials.

Other Group Processes

In our mobile society, many children are often faced with moving to a new neighborhood, learning their way around a new city, meeting new people, and making new friends. Teachers can help students recognize the wide range of feelings associated with adapting to new situations, help students develop support for one another, and help them develop the social skills they will need to be successful in dealing with these changes—which often can be traumatic. Similarly, other personal or community issues can be addressed through group activities.

Small groups or a fishbowl structure (in which a small number of students are selected to sit in the middle of the room while the remaining students observe) can facilitate discussion of such topics as peer pressure, gender roles, dealing with parents, school traditions, or problems in the community.

Notational-Functional Approach

One of the most recent approaches to language learning, the notational-functional approach, first identifies the communication needs of students and then structures lessons around those needs. The social situations (home, work, leisure activities, transportation, health facilities, and the like) and social roles are identified. Then the concepts (time, money, etc.) related to those settings are ordered for presentation. Vocabulary and grammar are then integrated as the student learns the functions of language—for example, how to make a statement, ask a question, make a comparison, or express feelings.

The notational-functional approach helps the regular classroom teacher become aware of the language skills students need for their daily lives. Language related to school and the community will be of primary importance. The teacher will need to assess which skills students possess and which they need to acquire. For example:

1. Can they introduce themselves?

2. Can they follow street directions?

3. Can they fill out forms?

4. Can they ask for help?

5. Can they read a menu?

6. Can they read and follow directions on medicine labels?

7. Can they make change with our currency?

8. Can they pass the driver's license test?

9. Do they understand commonly used idioms?

10. Do they know how to obtain social services?

With low-English-proficiency students, the classroom teacher may have to determine what language skills are most necessary for survival. A good way to begin is to focus on the roles of the students—student, family member, baby-sitter, dishwasher, athletic team player, and so on. Intermediate and advanced students can be asked what they need to know and to bring in examples. Role plays and simulations would be the corresponding models of teaching to implement. These tasks correlate well with social studies units in elementary school, but they will need extra attention at the secondary level.

Special attention can be given to signs in the community, information in the newspapers, ads on television and radio, and bulletins from church. Older students may need help with papers related to employment contracts and job benefits. Other topics might include leases, rental fees, and insurance.

A Review of Concepts

From each of the methods previously described, you can use the following review chart as a reference for planning lessons using strategies adopted from second-language approaches for your limited-English students.

Summary of Strategies
Adapted From Teaching Second Languages

1. Teach English through content.

2. Choose suitable vocabulary.

3. Identify words as part of culture.

4. Use high-interest, high-context topics.

5. Expose limited-English students to basic vocabulary.

6. Recognize stages of speech production.

7. Select questions according to ability.

8. Use total physical response.

9. Identify requests that are commonly made.

10. Check for comprehension by use of gestures, actions, and references to pictures or words on paper.

11. Provide a warm, relaxed environment.

12. Use relaxation techniques.

13. Incorporate music.

14. Read with different expressions.

15. Arrange seating in a circle for student conversation.

16. Acknowledge psychological and social needs.

17. Build trust and cooperation.

18. Use group activities as much as possible.

19. Let students talk about what is important to them.

20. Assess and teach language skills needed for daily living.

21. Identify students' social roles and social situations.

22. Use role-playing and simulation exercises.

23. Have students practice learning strategies and apply to a new task.

24. Organize objectives into short, meaningful, situation-oriented events.

25. Include periods for reflection.

Suggested Activities

1. Select a unit of study and identify the vocabulary that you would present to your students before introducing the unit. List the props, posters, and other visual aids you would use throughout the unit.

2. Listen to the speech of the students in your class and list the idioms you hear. Develop a language lesson around the use of idioms.

3. Select one of the methods developed by foreign language or English language teachers and develop a unit for your classroom.

4. Observe a teacher who has worked successfully with limited-English children in the classroom. Discuss the strategies demonstrated and the rationale behind them.

Chapter Six

Using Adjunct Structures

So much of a child's introduction to the English language comes not through formal schooling but through various media such as television, radio, popular music, computer games, and the Internet. Many of these adjunct structures can be used to support and strengthen work that takes place in the classroom.

Television

Children in many parts of the world have been known to surprise their parents by having learned English entirely from watching television, using the World Wide Web, and listening to popular music. "Our parents used to talk in English," an Icelander reports, "whenever they didn't want us kids to understand what they were talking about. But what they didn't realize is that we had picked up so much English just from watching comedy shows on television."

Among the best instructional devices, this Icelander found old reruns of *I Love Lucy* to be the absolute best English-teaching tool. "Lucy's face was so expressive and she used her whole body when she spoke, flailing her arms and contorting her face, that I could usually figure out what she was saying just from her gestures." The Icelander became thoughtful for a moment before continuing his story. Then he broke out into an uproarious laugh. "I just remembered something," he said with a giggle. After a bit of prompting, he continued. "Well, the one thing I could never figure out is why Lucy called her best friend 'asshole.' That just seemed so rude, especially for American TV which is so restricted."

"What are you talking about?" we prompted him, utterly confused by what he was talking about. Lucille Ball would never have used a swear word like that, especially in the 1950s.

"Well," he explained, snickering, "it took me the longest time to figure out that Lucy's best friend wasn't really 'Asshole,' but 'Ethel.' They sure sounded the same to me."

Indeed, just imagine all the mistakes in understanding that people make when they are learning English from the media. Nevertheless, watching soap operas, music videos, and situation comedies is among the best ways for students to sensitize themselves to English sounds and usage.

Using Technology

A variety of equipment is available to classroom teachers that you will find useful in working with limited-English students. Cassette tape recorders, videotape recorders, televisions, telephones, and computers can all be utilized to help individualize and personalize your instruction.

Tape Recorders

There are many ways to use tape recorders in the classroom. To begin with, you can tape your presentations for students to play back at a later time. Students then have the opportunity to digest small bits of information at a time. It is a good way to have students work on pronunciation. For example, after hearing new words or phrases, they can say them aloud and then compare their expression with yours: "I pledge allegiance . . . to the flag . . . of the United States . . . of America."

You can tape-record questions for those students who can't read or have trouble reading. In turn, they can answer on paper or tape-record their responses to you. Using the tape recorder will give them a chance to practice their answers. They can hear each answer and be sure it represents what they want to say. They can do a self-evaluation check.

You can prerecord material or special directions to go along with a textbook or other printed matter for those learning to read. Of course, there are many cassette-and-book sets of stories already available. By exchanging tapes you can build a special relationship with your students. Use it as a way to get to know about them. This practice will provide another vehicle for practicing their language skills. Working with a tape recorder will allow you to individualize your lessons. You can prepare material for preview, review, practice, or enrichment.

Video

Many school districts have sophisticated equipment available for student use. By videotaping a presentation for later playback, you will enable the student to see demonstrations and examples that were part of a presentation. Again, the student can follow the lesson at his or her own pace.

Students can use videotape to carry out assignments and develop creative projects. For example, they can research the amount of graffiti in the streets, or the number of people using public transportation can be shown on a screen, allowing the limited-English speaker to be involved in activities and carry out research that does not rely on reading skills.

Videotape can also be used to record progress. Periodic taping of students' involvement in activities will allow the students to see how language skills are progressing. By viewing the videotape with supervision, the student can also become aware of his or her body language and evaluate its appropriateness.

Telephone

In checking for comprehension and developing social skills, consider exercises using the telephone. Students can call for information from prerecorded messages. For example, time and weather information can be obtained by telephone. Movie information is also available. Have students plan a trip and obtain airplane arrival and departure times, weather information, hours of operation, locations, and prices.

Computer Applications

With the development of computer technology, most children will have the opportunity to use computers in the classroom. Computers not only stimulate motivation but also offer a variety of activities. Students can work individually, in pairs, or even in small groups. They work at their own pace on self-directed projects. Students take great pride in the work they print from the computer. Students can publish books, stories, and reports. They can produce banners, cards, and posters.

Supportive and Instructional Software

For those just beginning to learn English, drawing programs such as Kid Pix allow students to combine graphics with labeling, building up vocabulary, and spelling. Or students can scan their own drawings into the computer and import them into whatever software they are using. The illustrated words and terms can then be used as the basis for sentences and later, when students are more advanced, for writing stories and reports. Other suggestions for using pictures as stimuli to encourage students to respond are presented in Chapter 4 in the section on drawing.

For young students, there are software programs now available to introduce letters and words. Such programs will be helpful with students beginning to read. There are games, puzzles, and drills as well as stories to provide practice. Reksten (2000) suggests using computer programs to reinforce math skills as students represent numbers with objects.

Typing tutorials help students develop the keyboard skills they need. There are writing programs to help students through the composing process. Students can create plays, surveys, interviews, poetry, letters to pen pals, and newspapers. For more advanced students, desktop publishing programs will enhance newspaper production with the use of graphics.

Reksten (2000) recommends that students as early as kindergarten learn to select and use software programs to type numbers, letters, words, and sentences and to draw pictures to illustrate their ideas. At the first-grade level, students can use multimedia software, such as PowerPoint or Hyperstudio, to demonstrate sequencing of story. Pictures, text, or both can be ordered chronologically by the students in sequential frames. Children can also create their own stories in this way.

Word Processing

Students should be able to continue their computer skills with word processing and graphics. As writing increases, students can use editing features for spell-checking, grammar correction, and formatting. Also, production software, such as Classroom Publisher, allows students to produce newsletters. As keyboarding skills improve, students will be able to type more quickly and accurately.

The word-processing capabilities of computers allow students to concentrate on what they are trying to say without being bogged down by the slowness of handwriting, erasing, and correcting or by looking words up in the dictionary. The features of spell-checking, thesaurus, and grammar-checking alleviate the worry of the technical aspects of writing. The limited-English students receive the support they need in order to express ideas.

Desktop publishing software, such as Adobe Pagemaker, offers a unique opportunity for students to build their own dictionaries with graphics. As they become more proficient, they can create their own projects, from posters to newspapers. They can create electronic dictionaries and encyclopedias. Other projects might include creative writing magazines, school handbooks, instruction manuals, yearbooks, catalogs, and calendars. The possibilities are endless. These activities give students opportunities to develop and practice not only reading and writing skills but also the social skills needed for collaboration.

Word processing can also be used to help students learn to read using the language experience approach described in the previous chapter. As their words are keyed into the computer by others, students come into contact with meaningful print. They will be encouraged to continue writing, or in this case typing on the keyboard, in a purposeful manner to increase their reading skills.

Electronic Mail

With electronic mail capability, your students can communicate with others all over the world. They will have an audience for their writing. Whether to exchange letters, to seek information, or to be involved in collecting information for a group scientific study, electronic mail can open the doors of your classroom by promoting active inquiry.

The whole concept of "pen pals" has been made so routine that students can easily communicate with dozens of friends in every part of the world. Some teachers have combined such vehicles with video conferencing between classrooms so that students can actually see the people with whom they are communicating. This structure works especially well when students from foreign countries are able to arrange partnerships with their schools back home.

Reading Support

Reader software, such as Arkenstone's WYNN (What You Need Now) reader or CAST's eReader, allow text material to be scanned into a computer. Then students can follow the print as it is read aloud. A middle school teacher explains:

> While this takes a considerable amount of time to begin with, once the task is complete, it can be used over and over again. I found that graphs and charts and pictures did not scan well, so I just used text for my students. This made a great difference for my ELL students.

It is easy for the teacher to include special directions, point out new words that students will encounter, and preview the section before the students begin the actual reading. You can link the new material to what has been previously studied and emphasize the important ideas or significant events. This program also allows students to change the presentation. They can edit, highlight, and take notes.

Databases

For all students, creating database programs will give them the chance to collect and analyze information as part of a science or social studies project. Students can generate hypotheses, collect and record information, and evaluate the results as they explore the world they live in. Data can be gathered by observation, survey, or interview. The type and amount of information collected will need to be carefully structured by the teacher so as not to be overwhelming or unmanageable. Older and more proficient students can move beyond categorization to develop their own research questions and determine how they will collect the information they need. Databases also store information that students can retrieve as they study a particular subject for an oral or written report.

Using spreadsheets is another way to handle information. These can be used in mathematics lessons, because they allow mathematical operations to be performed through the addition of formulas. Lessons can then be combined with graphing exercises. Students can observe changes taking place in real or simulated exercises.

Critical Thinking

New software supports the development of critical thinking. For development of chronology, Tom Snyder's TimeLiner provides students with the ability to create annotated time lines. The makers of the program Inspiration continue to upgrade software for brainstorming and sequencing information. Map-making programs are also available.

LOGO is a list programming language that has been successful with abstract mathematical concepts and numeracy. Students move a robot in the shape of a turtle around a piece of paper by specifying what direction to move and how far to move in degrees. Immediately, students see the result of their programming. Students are forced to confront errors and identify possible alternative solutions, thus gaining experience in problem solving as well as cause-and-effect relationships. With LOGO, students progress from developing spatial skills to higher-level skills of geometry. Other mathematical programs are available that allow students to explore the dynamic relationships of math concepts.

Presentation software, such as PowerPoint, allows students "to put it all together." As a culminating activity for a unit of study, students can present results of research or an experiment with a slide show that includes graphics and pictures as well as text. Children with limited English can be active participants in team projects with the responsibility of creating slides to include in a presentation.

Palm computers give students the opportunity to manipulate information. From graphic calculators to the new handheld computers, technology offers new tools. Patterson (2000) describes software, such as ImagiMath, that helps students to see graphing solutions and then to be able to print them. Science probe attachments, such as ImagiWorks, enable students to go into the field and take measurements that can be analyzed at a later date. Students enter data from observations and then upload information to a computer to create databases. Software programs also allow students to store great quantities of information.

Digital Photography

The increasing availability of digital cameras, both still and video, offers students additional ways to be creative in conducting research and presenting their results. In science, for example, they can capture the growth of plants and incorporate the pictures into a report. In social studies, students with digital cameras can capture events as they occur, such as interviews or public events, or they can produce skits for later viewing.

Using the Internet

With teacher guidance, students can use the Internet as a source of reference information. They can download text, pictures, graphs, and charts for use in reports or pictures to illustrate stories. They can also communicate with others throughout the Internet. Finally, students can share the results of what they have learned.

Beginning at the fourth- or fifth-grade level, students can be taught to create Web pages. With additional technology training, they can display their projects and reports as well as contribute to a school Web site.

New Web quests and interactive projects are announced all the time for use in a variety of content areas. Students are presented with a question and use the Internet to find the answer in inquiry-based learning activities. Classroom Connect's The Quest Channel provides an inquiry-based online field trip. Particularly popular in 2000 with the Olympics in Sydney was *AustraliaQuest*. Students can learn how the stock market functions by participating in one of the online stock market games.

The JASON Project is a nationally known science program with an extensive Web site. This program was founded by Robert Ballard, explorer and oceanographer known for discovering the wreck of the *Titanic*. Each year students are able to travel to a different place in the world and follow the scientists in their work through virtual field trips. During two weeks each spring the expedition is beamed via satellite to participating sites in live broadcasts.

Simulations

For years students have participated in the Stock Market Game™, a "real-life" simulation of investment. Students compete against other teams and invest an initial $100,000 in common stocks during a 10-week trading session. Students learn about the U.S. economy as they execute the steps to buy and sell shares of stock, identify criteria for evaluating a business, identify different forms of business, and identify the sources of funds available to these businesses.

The significance of using the latest technologies in the classroom is that they support the delivery of content in all curriculum areas if selected for the appropriate grade level. The virtual manipulation of objects and information allows students to proceed at the appropriate academic level when language skills may be below level. The Internet provides an instant source of information to students in a variety of languages. There are Web sites for translations, too.

Other Resources

We hope that the strategies presented in this chapter will give you many ideas to try in your own classroom. Remember, you are not alone. The next chapter discusses other resources that are available to you and how to involve others in the classroom.

Suggested Activities

1. Select a topic of study and identify all the technological adjuncts you could incorporate into the lesson to help the limited-English students.

2. Evaluate where your students are in their development of technology skills. Plan a technology-related lesson that will offer them the opportunity to use their skills as they become involved with the content you are presenting.

3. Research Web sites that would be good sources of information for your students. As one example, visit the Internet at www.eslcafe.com to access Dave Sperling's Web site, Dave's ESL Café. Visit or join a forum on elementary or secondary education.

4. Make plans to get specialized training in instructional technology in order to develop other ways that you can capitalize on various media to support your teaching efforts.

Chapter Seven

Involving Others

"It's not a globe, it's a balloon," said one student to another.
"Let me show you how to blow it up."

W hen the teacher heard the previous segment of a conversation, she realized she was not the only person from whom her students would be learning English. There would be many "helping teachers" who would introduce new concepts, model pronunciation, and make corrections when necessary.

Because children learn as much English, if not more, from their peers as they do from the planned curriculum, teachers can capitalize on this natural phenomenon in systematic ways. This chapter will highlight many of the ways you can utilize the resources of other people, from children in the classroom and school personnel to people in the community, in efforts to facilitate language acquisition.

Peer Instruction

Sometimes teachers forget that some of the most significant learning that takes place in school is neither in the classroom nor mediated by professional educators. You would only have to think back to your own learning experiences that had the most impact to recall that most of them occurred on the playground, in the lunchroom, during hall passes, and mostly during supposed play time with friends and schoolmates. Often these were lessons about sharing, friendship, and loyalty, but occasionally they covered the realities of betrayal, intimidation, and fear. Regardless of the case, there is little doubt that agemates and peer pressure often have considerably more influence on student behavior than do the best intentions of teachers.

It is a wise teacher who recognizes the power of peer interactions and seeks to capitalize on this influence to promote learning objectives. As an example, when a 10th-grade student is asked his favorite class in school, he doesn't even hesitate to reply, "Spanish."

"Spanish?"

"Kinda surprised, aren't you?" he replies with a grin.

This boy is an athlete and is not known for his academic interests. Puzzled, you investigate further, asking him to elaborate. What you discover is that he absolutely loves Spanish class because the teacher gives kids the opportunity to talk to each other, if they can manage to do so using Spanish and a modified sign language.

For any number of reasons, children often learn best from one another, especially in situations when they don't feel critically judged. After all, where do kids learn about life's most important lessons—such as sex, love, and friendship—except from one another? And where else do they learn about language?

Buddy System

In order to help new students feel comfortable, one obvious structure would be to assign a designated partner as a guide to aid adjustment. This helper would be ideally positioned to give encouragement and to make sure the student has the right supplies and follows directions given to the class. Of equal importance, the new arrival will have a companion, someone to interact with throughout the day. In addition, "buddies" also profit from their experience as helpers. They learn what it means to be responsible in carrying through commitments. Their relationships with the teacher will be enhanced as they realize they were selected (or volunteered) for this responsibility. They learn the joy of explaining things to others in a way the others finally understand. In fact, many of us were "born" as teachers when we were given opportunities as children to help our peers and siblings. Many of us can recall what a privilege it was to be chosen to escort another student to the office! Not only were we the ones chosen from the entire class, but we were also released from the discipline codes of "Stay in your seat" and "No talking."

Studies of conversations show that children are quite different from teachers when they point out mistakes to their peers. Children focus on the social aspect, asking for clarification only when they cannot understand what is communicated. Teachers, however, attend to the content, rectify the mistake, and expect the child to use the correct response in the future. This, of course, can be a humiliating experience for children who are trying hard to please a new teacher in a new culture. One obvious example of this occurs when assignments are read aloud. Children who are struggling to pronounce a word are quite grateful for the assistance of a peer, yet when the teacher corrects them, they often feel censured.

With elementary students, another approach is to assign different buddies for different tasks. This widens the exposure of students without overwhelming any single individual. For example, one student might be assigned as a "study buddy," a second student would function as a "lunch buddy" to take the student to the cafeteria, and a third student would be a "bus buddy" to make sure the student gets on the right bus and has a person to sit with.

Each of the helpers is given an opportunity to develop a sense of responsibility and leadership skills. The experience also helps each buddy develop empathy, as he or she feels the experience of one who is different. With each assistant the teacher recruits, he or she is also able to create a new bond in the ongoing relationship with students. It is as if the teacher is saying, "I trust you. I value your help. I feel grateful for your willingness to pitch in and help. We are all trying to learn together."

Team Teaching

Rarely are you the only teacher a student comes in contact with during the day. Integrating the curriculum across disciplines is extremely helpful for students with limited English. When this is done, the teachers are able to target the vocabulary and grammar they are using. Principles are reinforced throughout the day. You can develop your own themes or use commercially prepared kits in which English and social studies skills are combined with science and math concepts.

Although it might be optimistic to expect all the teachers to coordinate their efforts, it may be more practical to coordinate intentions with a few with whom you have good rapport. For example, an elementary teacher can make sure that the librarian and art teacher are aware of what has been taking place and what they can do to help. Even the bus driver can be recruited to pitch in: "When Tasha comes on the bus, ask her slowly how her day was. Then please make sure she does not sit alone."

Many schools are now implementing teaming or are providing teachers with coordinated planning time and shared students structured into their schedules. Most important, secondary teachers must communicate with one another on a regular basis so that progress is not restricted to a single class or compartmentalized in such a way that the student becomes confused with inconsistencies or overwhelmed by vocabulary. For example, a social studies teacher can combine forces with the math teacher to reinforce the concept of angles in studying the pyramids of ancient Egypt. On a more general level, several teachers can get together and coordinate their efforts: "I notice that Ling really cringes when I attempt to correct him. What have you tried that works better? Maybe we could all try to do the same thing so that he hears consistent feedback."

Imagine how frustrated a limited-English student would be if she were told by one teacher to do or say one thing, while another required something else, and still another quite another thing. For example, a student is encouraged by one teacher to talk as much as possible and not worry about grammar; another teacher tells him to exercise more restraint and only speak after he has thought through what he wants to say and how he will say it; a third teacher absolutely insists that he not speak at all until he can "talk right." With these mixed messages, such a student is likely to follow the advice of the third teacher, avoiding the risk of making mistakes whenever possible.

Special School Personnel

There may be additional resource people available in your school or in your district for collaboration. One such specialist is the ELL teacher. Generally, nonproficient children are placed in an ELL class for part of the day and in the regular classroom for the rest of the time. The number of hours varies depending on the school district and the needs of the students. The dynamics of the ELL class may be far different from the way you might usually structure your own class.

You may be able to coordinate with the ELL teacher on the vocabulary of the subject you teach. Another approach is for the ELL teacher to use sheltered English to teach a content area. If you contact the ELL teacher in your area and correlate your classroom teaching lessons, he or she can prepare the student by introducing needed background concepts before you present new material. In addition, the ELL teacher can introduce related vocabulary. If you notice mistakes in grammar or pronunciation, you can communicate them to the ELL teacher, who can work with the student individually in particular areas, allowing you to address other matters. By coordinating your efforts, you will eliminate duplication and not subject the student to undue pressure.

Although being placed in ELL classes offers special instruction and an opportunity to meet with like peers, it also has some disadvantages. Students often complain that they don't like being identified as different. Pulling them out of their regular classrooms may make them feel as if they are falling even further behind or missing shared experiences with the other students. Furthermore, they are limited in hearing English as spoken by their peers. It is helpful to be aware of the awkward situation these students find themselves in and the mixed emotions they experience.

Again, coordinating with other professionals can help to minimize some of these problems. For example, you might say, "I notice that Hassan leaves class reluctantly when it is time to meet with you.

It seems as if he does not want to make up more work that he missed. If in your work with him you could combine some of my tasks with your own, he would not feel as reluctant."

Other possible sources of support would be bilingual teachers, foreign language teachers, and English teachers in your school or in your district. They might be willing to share strategies and materials with you, or you could invite them to visit your classroom and make suggestions specific to identified students. Outside the classroom, you could ask them to help you brainstorm strategies to use in delivering specific content.

If a student receives a reading score below a given level on a standardized test, the student is entitled to help from a reading resource teacher. Once again, rather than have the reading teacher work in isolation from the regular classroom, you can discuss your units with the reading teacher so that he or she can prepare the student to participate in the regular classroom. This professional will be dealing not only with reading skills per se but also with writing, speaking, and listening. The student can practice with the reading teacher privately before being called on in front of a group of peers or the whole class.

Traditionally, the reading teacher has worked with students in a "pull-out" situation in a room outside the regular classroom. However, rather than isolating students, reading teachers are beginning to work right in the regular classroom. This provides the reading teacher with the opportunity to see how the regular classroom, and the teacher in particular, function. It is also less disruptive for the students, who are often afraid (rightfully so) they are going to miss something "fun" or "important" when they are called out of class.

Special education teachers can also be a resource. They have experience in making modifications for students. They can help you determine if reduced assignments or extra time for testing would be in order. They may suggest calculator usage or word processing as an aid. They may help you with physical changes in the classroom, such as preferential seating, and can help you develop behavior plans based on the actions of the students. They may also have resources to help you, such as talking board pictures. They can also help you determine when structural approaches are helpful. For example, one special education teacher notes,

I had two Vietnamese students who were having trouble with conversational phrases. They could memorize them but did not use them. So, I sat down with them and explained the parts of speech—subjects and predicates. Then, the girls were able to make connections with their own languages and quickly mastered the phrases.

Other personnel to consult with would include the school counselor, social worker, and psychologist. They can offer aid in the areas of handling adjustment, building self-esteem, and establishing support groups. They can also deal with issues related to fear of failure, perfectionist attitudes, and other cognitive messages that interfere with learning.

In one application of counseling theory called "cognitive interventions," students are taught to monitor their internal thinking processes and change the way they talk to themselves inside their heads. If a student says to herself "I'm stupid" every time she makes a mistake, this is going to be very inhibiting to her learning English (or anything else). Instead of being so hard on herself, she can be taught to substitute, "I'm human and I only made a mistake." Some other examples are as follows:

What a Student Thinks	Alternative Thoughts
"I am the *only* one who has problems."	"Others are struggling as well."
"This is *awful* that I messed up."	"This is only a minor setback."
"This *should* be easy."	"This is a real challenge for me."
"I'll *never* get this stupid language."	"I will learn English in time."

In addition, counselors can help you work directly with students in addressing emotional needs. We often forget to look at the big picture, how struggles with school work and language skills affect every other facet of a child's life. When needed, referrals can be made to other resources in the community.

For example, in the case of one child who was struggling not only with learning English but also with staying out of the reach of his alcoholic, abusive father, a school counselor was instrumental in helping to stabilize the family situation. Efforts by the principal, school psychologist, counselor, and referring teacher were all united in their determination to help this child succeed in spite of adverse conditions.

When this child was later able to express himself more fully, he explained to his teacher that as much as he appreciated the help he received with his school performance and language abilities, of even greater importance was the interaction that helped change the poisonous atmosphere of his home. If these American people seemed to care enough to intervene on his behalf, surely he could learn their language so that he might thank them.

One last group of school personnel who offer a specialized area of expertise are the speech teachers. They can offer suggestions related to pronunciation, but remember, for some students, it will be difficult to speak a new language without an accent if they are above the age of 12 or 13 when they begin to learn. Some students will never lose their accents.

Cross-Age Tutoring

Another type of project that has met with success is a tutoring program. As older and experienced students are paired with younger students, benefits to both parties accrue. For students who have recently arrived in this country, there is much comfort in meeting someone who can identify with the experience of being immersed in a new culture and who understands how problems arise. Older students can empathize and share what they did and how it helped them. They also serve as role models. One such program might involve setting up a system whereby junior high or high school students meet once a week with early elementary school students. The older students are given the responsibility to plan for and prepare an hour of activity.

Tutoring sessions require planning and coordination by both teachers. For example, the older students can be responsible for implementing activities related to a unit being studied in the regular classroom. Students might work in groups or be paired individually. Their activities might include reading to younger children, sight word instruction, or word puzzles. Hearing-sound activities can include reading Dr. Seuss's books to attain phonemic awareness. Letter-sound activities can involve putting up letters for a known word and changing the first letter (*run* to *sun* to *fun*). Writing activities can include writing books or letters together. The tutors, under the supervision of the teachers, would have to decide what activities would be appropriate, which materials they would need, and how to structure the time spent with the students.

This presents a problem-solving situation that involves higher-level thinking skills for the tutors. The tutors would have to analyze their own learning and break it down into steps for the younger students. These activities would serve also as a reinforcement for the older students. The tutors thus find themselves in a new role, as "teacher," which provides them with experience to help their own children in the future as they grow up.

They can also tutor students who are learning their native language. For example, Spanish speakers can work with native English-speaking students who are learning Spanish as an additional language. They can help with grammar as well as lessons on elements of culture. As peer models, the Spanish speakers can provide opportunities for other students to interact with native speakers. As another benefit, it may also serve as an introduction to a career in education.

The younger, less proficient students are placed in situations that are enjoyable and meaningful and that have low pressure. Remember, language is social in nature. In a tutoring situation, students are free to analyze their language skills and share strategies with each other. The older students can develop a sense of pride and accomplishment from helping others that can lead to an increase in self-esteem and the development of positive attitudes about themselves and school. Studies show that tutors gain in achievement and attitude, giving credence to the idea, "If you want to learn something, teach it!"

Parents

As we have mentioned earlier, it is especially important for parents to be involved in activities that support literacy. Teachers can provide parents with examples of activities they can do at home. Many districts offer sessions for parents during the day and in the evenings. Reading to young children in any language and talking about the reading are vital activities that support fluency of communication. Those parents who are literate, but not in English, can be encouraged to read to their children in their native language. Teachers can impress on the parents their responsibility to pass their heritage (folk tales, rhymes, and poetry) from one generation to the next. The recently developed "Proyecto Futuro" identifies science experiments that can be done at home with objects commonly found around the house. Handouts are provided with Spanish on one side and English on the other.

Teachers can also explain to parents how children learn as well as the type of behavior expected by the teacher in the classroom. The problem is that teachers receive so little training in how to consult with parents. What do you do with a parent who is resistant to your best efforts? How do you handle the parent who feels you are meddling? What do you do when there are obvious family problems that are affecting the child's behavior? How do you get parents to comply with what you are suggesting?

In an ideal situation, counseling specialists would be available to address these difficulties. Alas, such help is not often available, leaving you with the task. Because you may feel unprepared to apply advanced-level helping skills, you can recruit the assistance of experts to help train you and others who are interested (see Kottler, 2000; Kottler & Kottler, 2000, as resources). Faculty at the university can recommend books for you to read and can design workshops for you in this area that would teach you strategies to use in consulting with parents.

In one school, a teacher who was taking some counseling classes put together a miniworkshop for parents who were interested in augmenting their skills in parenting. These sessions ran four weeks at a time and covered such topics as opening lines of communication with your child, setting limits, balancing school and outside activities, and when to seek outside help for family problems.

Participating in parent-teacher organizations is another way to get to know and enlist the support of the parents of your community. Your visibility in such associations is proof that you are working with the parents to provide the best education possible for their children.

Intergenerational Tutoring

Adults of retirement age are able to offer a wealth of skills and knowledge. Many cultures value group interaction. Intergenerational tutoring is an extension that naturally fits into the public school arena. There are many parents and grandparents who will volunteer their time to help students. Also, they can read to students or have students read to them. They can offer explanations or translations as appropriate. They can do demonstrations and give additional examples for individuals or small groups. The teacher needs only to match the adult with the student and provide appropriate activities.

Community Resources

Open the doors to your classroom. Venture out or bring the world inside your room to provide immediate experiences for your students. Anyone who has become truly fluent in another language did not learn it in the classroom. Once you get students excited about learning English, they will be motivated to take what they have learned into the real world where it really counts.

As with most learning, motivation is a key. If students see a reason why mastering English is one key to their life satisfaction and success, your only job will be to structure their learning, because wild horses couldn't hold them back. If you have ever traveled in a foreign country where you couldn't communicate your basic needs, it did not take much incentive for you to learn, "Where is the toilet?" People have a habit of learning what they need most to get what they want.

Field Trips

Expand the classroom by taking a field trip to a farm, factory, or post office. For some students, the bus ride through the community alone is an eye-opening experience. You would be surprised how many students have never left their neighborhoods.

Visiting restaurants of different ethnic groups is a popular field trip. Decor, food, background music, and in some cases foreign menus give students an indication of different customs. Visiting museums to see traveling exhibitions can also be a meaningful trip. It is important for all students to see contributions made by people of diverse backgrounds.

Visitors

There are many people in the community who may be willing to visit your classroom. Invite businesspeople to come and demonstrate the services they provide or the products they produce, as they relate to topics of study, to bring these subjects alive for the students. The subject of owning a business can be a lesson in itself. Many people will bring samples for the students. The visit can serve as an introductory or culminating activity for a unit. Students can prepare a list of questions ahead of time. Homemakers have talents or hobbies as well that they can share with your students. Asking members of your students' families to talk about their work or avocation will create bonds in the classroom. You don't have to wait for Career Day or Culture Day. These can be ongoing visits.

Imagine a renowned chef coming to class bearing samples of the masterpieces she has created, letting the children taste her treats, and explaining how she creates new dishes. Then, she describes her own life story, how when she first arrived in this country and stepped off the boat, she could not speak a word of English.

She says she felt as if she were invisible, that as long as she could not speak the language of this country, nobody would give her a chance. She was determined, however, that she would speak English like a native (the kids laugh because she has a thick accent). "Okay, okay, so I don't speak so good." (The kids laugh again.) "Well, I don't speak well. Better? Anyway, English is everything to be successful. What good is it to cook like an angel if I can't talk to other people? All of you, not just those of you from other countries, must study hard in school. Your whole life, people will judge you by the way you speak." What an effective presentation that would be!

Artists, musicians, skilled craftspeople, and scientists could present their work to students of any level. Again, it would be particularly meaningful if the guests spoke English as a second language.

On the secondary level, for more proficient students you can consider inviting guests to talk about their personal experiences on key concepts such as acculturation, immigration, prejudice, political power, and social conditions in our society. Again, they can share their unique stories and contributions to our society.

Cultural Exchanges

Art, music, dress, and foods can be the central themes of a multicultural awareness experience. Potluck lunches or dinners bring together people of the community. Students can be assigned to give an informative talk, sing a song, demonstrate a dance, explain a game, write a recipe, or prepare a dish. Students or adults can show pictures or slides of places they have lived or traveled and talk about the customs there.

Language for All

Although this book emphasizes teaching strategies for individuals with differences in their language capacities, children are very similar in their basic desires. They want to understand the world around them. They want to be accepted and liked by their peers. They want to develop skills and knowledge that will help them be successful in life. They want to feel validated by their teachers. Through the strategies presented in this book, it is possible for teachers to be more sensitive to the children in their care.

In spite of your best intentions to be more responsive to children who are struggling as newcomers to our culture and language, there are limits on the time, energy, and resources that you have available. Even though you may be overburdened with other responsibilities and priorities, even though you don't feel adequately prepared to handle many of the challenges you will face with limited-English students, you can make a difference in a relatively short period of time.

Suggested Activities

1. Make a catalog of possible speakers with culturally diverse backgrounds who could make presentations to your students.

2. Identify potential field trip sites that would expand the experiences of your students.

3. List possible resource personnel in your school or district that you could team with for consultation.

4. Plan an integrated interdisciplinary unit with a colleague for students with limited English.

5. Learn some basic counseling skills (such as "active listening") in order to sensitize yourself better to nuances in expressed communication and to respond more effectively to students' emotional needs.

Chapter Eight

Putting It All Together

The concepts and skills presented in this book provide you with some of the basics you need to implement programs and structures helpful to the students in your classroom who are struggling the most. Now it is time to put everything we covered together in some sort of organized framework.

Recent research on brain functioning as it relates to learning is one useful integrative model. We begin with a review of the brain research that relates in particular to working with limited-English children in the classroom, examine the research on indicators of effective schooling, and conclude with general guidelines to help get you started.

Examining the Classroom
Implications of Brain Research

Educators have been following closely the results of current brain research to see how they can make use of new findings. The new technologies of the 1990s, such as magnetic resonance imaging, positron emission tomography, and magnetoencephalography, to name a few, have increased our knowledge of how the brain functions. When this is added to recent advances in the understanding of neurotransmitters and brain chemistry, a clearer picture has emerged of how the brain learns.

Recent findings may be summarized as follows (Sousa, 2001):

- Past experience affects new learning. It is important to activate prior knowledge before introducing new concepts. This means using the students' experiences as examples of what you teach.

- The brain is always changing based on new experiences. This process is known as *neuroplasticity*. Teachers should provide educational experiences that will be somewhat challenging yet not too frustrating for students (Caulfield, Kidd, & Kocher, 2000).

- Both sides of the brain are involved in learning. Although the two hemispheres of the brain are specialized—the left side is logical in orientation, responsible for speech and analytical thinking, whereas the right side is intuitive in orientation, gathering information from images, responding to language through context, and processing information abstractly and holistically—people learn best when both hemispheres are involved. Lessons should be designed to include both verbal and visual concepts, to present both logical and intuitive concepts, and to give students options in terms of assessments that enable them to demonstrate what they know in a way that reflects their individual learning styles.

- A positive classroom environment promotes learning. Students need to feel comfortable in the classroom and to feel that they can express their opinions and have them respected. In order for this process to occur, you must take the time to build a trusting relationship with your students.

- Emotion plays a vital role in learning. If students like and are excited about what they learn, their interest will be maintained, and they will remember things more easily. They will also tend to move toward higher levels of thinking—analysis, synthesis, and evaluation. Novelty and humor play important roles in engaging students. Involvement and interaction are critical. Remember, as well, that lecturing is the *least* effective method to use in relation to students' retention of material.

- Students will respond differently based on their sensory preferences. Teachers need to provide experiences to address *all* sensory preferences and learning styles. In large classes, this is a very challenging task, considering all the other things that teachers must attend to. That doesn't mean it's impossible to individualize learning, only that it is difficult to do so (but we believe it is well worth it).

- The brain searches for meaning. Children with limited English need a *lot* of stimuli. As mentioned earlier, the importance of peer interaction cannot be stressed enough.

- Students can become aware of their thinking processes. Teach children metacognitive processes so that they become aware of what they know and how they learn.

- Provide time for reflection. Allow students a few minutes to review what they have learned. Take "time-outs" to make sense of what is being presented or learned.

In their review of the literature on effective programs for limited-English students, Samway and McKeon (1999) identify several indicators that are relevant to you as a classroom teacher. Three stand out in particular. First is establishing high expectations for students. Teachers must maintain their standards of achievement and hold all students accountable. Second, students need to interact with each other in meaningful ways. Language development occurs with academic development. Third, until conversation is possible, students are allowed to respond in their own language and have it translated when such support is available. These same ideas have been mentioned throughout the book. They are central, for example, to Freeman and Freeman's (1998) Principles for Success presented in Chapters 3 and 4.

A Review of Important Ideas

From classroom to classroom, learning takes place in a variety of ways. Although there is no magic wand to ensure that a smooth and speedy process will take place for the children with limited English, careful planning and preparation will provide you with the basis on which to structure a positive learning environment in which students will have the opportunity to succeed.

Educational Design

Plan reflectively and strategically what you want to do and how you intend to reach these goals (Dick & Carey, 1990; McTighe & Wiggins, 1998). Several steps are crucial.

Step 1. Determine your objectives. Whatever grade level you teach, from kindergarten through 12th grade, and whatever subject you teach, from core courses such as reading, science, mathematics, and social studies to elective courses such as vocational or fine arts, you need to identify your goals. What are the essential understandings? The big ideas? The sequence of skills? Begin by selecting what you want your students to know and be able to do. Consult your state standards and district frameworks or course syllabi for direction at this starting point.

Step 2. Select your assessment. The next stage is to identify how you will know what your students have learned and to what degree they have mastered the objectives you identified in Step 1. You may need to be creative with the assessments you choose depending on the level of proficiency of the limited-English speakers. You may consider offering a choice to students as to how they will demonstrate their knowledge or skill development, or you may even ask them to create the type of assessment.

In some cases, the traditional paper-and-pencil test will be easy and efficient to implement. However, you may find adaptations to be necessary, such as providing support with vocabulary boxes. You may consider recording the questions for students to follow along as they read and then ask them to indicate true or false or to select the best answer from a multiple choice.

Nontraditional forms will more likely be the assessment of choice, especially with beginning English students. For them, a drawing, sequencing project, or performance may be a more appropriate format. One-on-one interviews may help you best determine whether an understanding has been met. Following is a list of alternative assessments for your consideration:

- Diorama

- Mural

- Mobile

- Illustrated time line

- Story board

- Skit

- Illustrated map

- PowerPoint presentation

- Graph

- Chart

- Photo essay

- Portfolio display

- Reenactment

- Magazine or newspaper publication

- Poster of information

- Political cartoon

- Poem

- Skill demonstration

Consider your audience. Is there an individual or group with whom it would be appropriate for students to share their knowledge or show their skill development? Consider inviting a guest or guests to class such as principals, parents, community members, or other students.

Step 3. Assess the level of your students. Determine the entry level of your students. It is critical to determine their content background, previous school experiences, and language development. What prior knowledge and experiences will they need to have in order to be successful? Will you need to build experiences for them before they take on a new topic or begin a new reading? What vocabulary will they need to have before beginning a new concept? If you use a KWL chart, begin the K section. What do students already know, or what skills have they already mastered?

Step 4. Determine the learning activities. This is where the actual lesson planning takes place. Now is the time to decide on the methods of instruction you will use and the sequence of activities in which students will have the opportunity to practice new words and skills and apply new ideas.

Sousa (2001) suggests the following lesson design based on Madeline Hunter's (1982) model. Not all elements will be present in every lesson, but all should be included in every unit.

- *Anticipatory set.* Select a strategy that will get students' attention. It can range from showing a picture to telling a story to something humorous. The anticipatory set establishes the tone for the class period. It should relate to something students are familiar with and the objectives for the lesson.

If your students don't have the prerequisite background knowledge, you may need to "jump start" or provide an introductory minilesson by introducing vocabulary and reviewing concepts, showing pictures, or engaging in simulations or some sort of experiential activity (Echevarria et al., 2000). Depending on the numbers of students, you may choose to do this with a small group or with the entire class.

- *State the objective(s).* Include a description of what the assessment will be like. For limited-English students, avoid the "educationese" that is sometimes found in standards. The objectives need to be stated and written simply and clearly.

- *Give the purpose.* Explain why the students need to master the objective and explain how it relates to prior learning and future learning. Describe the whole picture. Students do not always make the connections on their own and need the teacher to show the links (Echevarria et al., 2000). This can easily be accomplished by referring to previous activities, reinforcing vocabulary, and graphic organizers.

- *Input.* Provide students with the information they need while addressing as many of the multiple intelligences as possible. This can take place in a variety of ways, from demonstrations, reading, lecture, and audiovisual presentations to student-conducted research, experiments, or presentations.

- *Modeling.* Show students clear examples to help them make sense of the new material. This is especially important for limited-English students. Modeling provides the scaffolding they need, the language prompts that will enable them to master new content.

- *Check for understanding.* Be sure students are making meaning of the new material by implementing any of a variety of techniques, from a "thumbs up, thumbs down" response, question and answer, discussion, a quiz, or a "think-pair-share" activity to a student-created graphic organizer.

- *Guided practice.* Provide ample time for students to review what they have learned and to apply it with immediate feedback to identify inaccuracies. These applications can be oral or written, ranging from summarizing in graphic organizers, writing in journals, creating posters, and solving problems to teaching another student. All these activities will promote retention.

- *Closure.* Enable students to summarize what they have learned. This can be an oral or written activity. Unit closure activities can include developing presentations, performing skits, writing original songs, or playing review games.

- *Independent practice.* Have students review what they have learned to increase retention. Rehearsal is essential.

Step 5. Gather resources and supplementary material. Identify textbook selections. Record or have someone else record selections for review and reinforcement. Choose the audiovisual aids you will need to support your lesson or unit. Gather your props—from puppets to artifacts. Make the charts, graphs, and multimedia presentations you will need for illustrations. Reserve the computer lab, if appropriate. List the materials for the science experiment. Pick out the manipulatives needed for the math activity. Flip the map holder to the correct map. Prepare graphic organizers, outlines, and study guides. Tape the text or adapt the text by rewriting complicated sections.

Step 6. Implement the lesson. It's time to begin. Provide the graphic organizer(s) and vocabulary support. Speak clearly and check for comprehension. Give students the opportunity to work with the problem or idea you present in small groups, or give them time to practice the new skill. Use the reading strategies mentioned in chapter 4 to facilitate reading comprehension.

As you walk around to observe and listen to students working, describe what you see so the limited-English students have the chance to hear your speech and to connect their actions and the objects they handle to words. Watch for nonverbal reactions that show students are confused or are having difficulty understanding. When observing small groups, watch to see if all group members participate. Provide ample time for practice and remediation.

Step 7. Evaluation. At the conclusion of the unit, give students the opportunity to demonstrate that they have mastered the objectives. Whether a formal test or a portfolio assessment, you will want to ask yourself the following questions: Were students successful? Could they demonstrate what they learned? Were they able to meet or exceed your expectations? What was surprising to you? What were the unanticipated obstacles and achievements? How did you feel about the lesson or unit? How was the pacing? What would you change if you were to do it again?

Your classroom will be a unique place in which you will learn from your students and they will learn from you. You will have the opportunity to develop relationships with your students and to observe the progress they make while in your class. Over time you will see your students master a new language as you improve your skills as a teacher. Perhaps the greatest gift you can ever offer to children, besides instilling a love of learning, is to help them express themselves in such a way that they are truly understood by others.

Suggested Activities

1. Incorporate the principles of brain research into one of your units. For example, chunk the material into meaningful segments, identify the appropriate metacognitive strategies you would have students implement, and plan time for reflection.

2. Consider the role of emotion in the learning, both as it relates to the classroom environment and as it applies to the readiness of individual learners to be successful.

3. Plan a new lesson or unit incorporating the implications of brain research and educational design theory.

4. Identify and monitor the effects of the changes in your teaching that you implement to determine their effectiveness. Experiment with new methods and observe the results.

5. Get together in small groups and talk about which ideas seem most useful to you based on what you read. Which ideas in the book do you disagree with most? Support your opinions with evidence from research, literature, and your own experiences.

References

Allington, R. L., & Cunningham, P. M. (1996). *Schools that work: Where all children read and write.* New York: Longman.

Atkinson, D. R., Morten, G., & Sue, D. W. (1997). *Counseling American minorities.* New York: McGraw-Hill.

Berry, J. W., & Sam, D. L. (1997). Acculturation and adaptation. In J. Berry, M. Segall, & C. Kagitcibasi (Eds.), *Cross-cultural psychology* (pp. 291-326). Boston: Allyn & Bacon.

Bowen, J. D., Madsen, H., & Hilferty, A. (1985). *TESOL techniques and procedures.* Cambridge, MA: Newbury House.

Burden, P. R. (2000). *Powerful classroom management strategies.* Thousand Oaks, CA: Corwin Press.

Cary, S. (2000). *Working with second language learners.* Portsmouth, NH: Heinemann.

Caulfield, J., Kidd, S., & Kocher, T. (2000). Brain-based instruction in action. *Educational Leadership, 58*(3), 62-65.

Chamot, A., & O'Malley, M. (1989). The Cognitive Academic Language Learning Approach. In P. Rigg & V. Allen (Eds.), *When they don't all speak English: Integrating the ESL student into the regular classroom* (pp. 108-125). Urbana, IL: National Council of Teachers of English.

Csikszentmihalyi, M. (1996). *Creativity: Flow and psychology of discovery and invention.* New York: HarperCollins.

Cummins, J. (1981). The role of primary language in promoting educational success for language minority students. In *Schooling and language minority students: A theoretical framework* (pp. 3-49). Los Angeles: Office of Bilingual Bicultural Education, California State University Evaluation, Dissemination, and Assessment Center.

Cummins, J. (1996). *Negotiating identities: Education for empowerment in a diverse society.* Ontario, CA: California Association of Bilingual Education.

Curan, C. (1976). *Counseling learning in second language.* Apple River, IL: Apple River Press.

Deschler, D. (1983). *Kephart symposis.* Paper presented at Kephart Symposia, Aspen, CO.

Dhority, L., & Jensen, E. (1998). *Joyful fluency: Brain-compatible second language acquisition.* San Diego, CA: The Brain Store.

Dick, W., & Carey, L. (1990). *The systematic design of instruction.* New York: HarperCollins.

Echevarria, J., Vogt, M., & Short, D. J. (2000). *Making content comprehensible for English Language Learners: The SIOP model.* Boston: Allyn & Bacon.

Freeman, Y. S., & Freeman, D. E. (1998). *ESL/EFL teaching: Principles for success.* Portsmouth, NH: Heinemann.

Gardner, H. (1983). *Frames of mind: A theory of multiple intelligences.* New York: Basic Books.

Gardner, H. (1993). *Creating minds.* New York: Basic Books.

Hazler, R. J. (1998). *Helping in the hallways: Advanced strategies for enhancing school relationships.* Thousand Oaks, CA: Corwin Press.

Herrell, A. (2000). *Fifty strategies for teaching English language learners.* Upper Saddle River, NJ: Merrill.

Hunter, M. (1982). *Mastery teaching.* El Segundo, CA: T.I.P. Publications.

Jensen, E. (1995). *Super teaching.* San Diego, CA: The Brain Store.

Johnson, D., & Johnson, R. (1998). *Learning together and alone* (5th ed.). Englewood Cliffs, NJ: Prentice Hall.

Kagan, S. (1994). *Cooperative learning.* San Juan Capistrano, CA: Kagan Cooperative Learning.

Kottler, J. A. (2000). *Nuts and bolts of helping.* Boston: Allyn & Bacon.

Kottler, J. A., & Kottler, E. (2000). *Counseling skills for teachers.* Thousand Oaks, CA: Corwin Press.

Kottler, J. A., & Zehm, S. (2000). *On being a teacher: The human dimension.* Thousand Oaks, CA: Corwin Press.

Krashen, S. (1996). *The natural approach: Language acquisition in the classroom* (Rev. ed.). Englewood Cliffs, NJ: Prentice Hall.

Lawrence, G., & Hunter, M. (1995). *Parent-teacher conferencing.* Thousand Oaks, CA: Corwin Press.

Lindsey, R. B., Nuri Robins, K., & Terrell, R. D. (1999). *Cultural proficiency: A manual for leaders.* Thousand Oaks, CA: Corwin Press.

Lozanov, G. (1979). *Suggestology and outlines of suggestopedia.* New York: Gordon and Breach.

MacDonald, S. (1998). *The portfolio and its use: A roadmap for assessment.* Beltsville, MD: Gryphon House.

McTighe, J., & Wiggins, G. (1998). *The understanding by design handbook.* Alexandria, VA: Association for Supervision and Curriculum Development.

Montgomery, M. (1999). *Building bridges with parents.* Thousand Oaks, CA: Corwin Press.

Nunan, D. (1999). *Second language teaching and learning.* Boston: Heinle & Heinle.

Nurss, J. R., & Hough, R. A. (1992). Reading and the ESL student. In S. J. Samuels & A. E. Farstrup (Eds.), *What research has to say about reading instruction* (pp. 277-307). Newark, DE: International Reading Association.

Ogle, D. (1989). The know, want to know, learn strategy. In K. D. Muth (Ed.), *Children's comprehension of text: Research into practice* (pp. 205-233). Newark, DE: International Reading Association.

Olson, L. (2001, January 10). Test debate: What counts as multiple? *Education Week, 1,* 18-19.

Patterson, J. C. (2000, December). A handheld primer. *Curriculum Administrator's Education in Hand,* 4-8.

Reksten, L. E. (2000). *Using technology to increase student learning.* Thousand Oaks, CA: Corwin Press.

Robinson, T. L., & Howard-Hamilton, M. F. (2000). *The convergence of race, ethnicity, and gender.* Columbus, OH: Merrill.

Rong, X. L. (1998). The new immigration: Challenges facing social studies professionals. *Social Education, 62,* 393-399.

Samway, K. D., & McKeon, D. (1999). *Myths and realities: Best practices for language minority students.* Portsmouth, NJ: Heinemann.

Santa, C. M., Havens, L. T., & Maycumber, E. M. (1996). *Project CRISS: Creating independence through student-owned strategies.* Dubuque, IA: Kendall/Hunt.

Scarcella, R. (1990). *Teaching language minority students in the multicultural classroom.* Englewood Cliffs, NJ: Prentice Hall Regents.

Schurr, S. (1999). *Authentic assessment: Using product, performance, and portfolio measures from A to Z.* Westerville, OH: National Middle School Association.

Seely, C., & Romijn, E. (1995). *TPR is more than commands: At all levels.* Berkeley, CA: Command Performance Language Institute.

Sharan, Y., & Sharan, S. (1992). *Expanding cooperative learning through group investigation.* New York: Teachers College Press.

Slavin, R. (1988). *Student team learning: An overview and practical guide.* Washington, DC: National Education Association.

Sousa, D. (2001). *How the brain learns.* Thousand Oaks, CA: Corwin Press.

Thomas, W. P., & Collier, V. (1997). *School effectiveness for language minority students.* Washington, DC: National Clearinghouse for Bilingual Education.

Timm, J. (1996). *Four perspectives in multicultural education.* New York: Wadsworth.

U.S. Department of Immigration and Naturalization Service. (1999). *Office of policy and planning statistics branch annual report* (No. 2). Washington, DC: Author.

Index

Acculturation, 18-19
Acronyms, 60
Activities, multisensory, 70-74
Age, language development and, 47
Allington, R. L., 22, 132
Analytic learning style, 65
Anxiety-free atmosphere, 63, 87
Art, as teaching tool, 72-73
Asher, J., 86
Assessment, 50, 126-128
Atkinson, D. R., 19, 132
Auditory learning modality, 65, 71

Ballard, R., 107
Berry, J. W., 19, 132
Bilingual adults:
    for community-language learn-
        ing, 87
    involvement in classroom, 29-31
Bilingual dictionaries, 76
Bilingual students, use of term, 5
Bilingual Syntax Measure, 50
Bilingual teachers, 87, 114
Bodily-kinesthetic intelligence, 69
Bowen, J. D., 86, 132
Brain, neuroplasticity, 124
Brain research, learning impacted by,
    124-126
Buddy system, 31-33, 110-112
Burden, P. R., 58, 132

CALLA. *See* Cognitive Academic
    Language Learning Approach
CALP. *See* Cognitive academic lan-
    guage proficiency
Carey, L., 126, 133
Cary, S., 5, 74, 79, 132
Caulfield, J., 126, 132
Chamot, A., 88, 89, 132
Children with limited English:
    use of term, 5-6
    See also Second-language devel-
        opment; Students
Classroom environment, 25-39

anxiety-free atmosphere, 63, 87
bilingual adults for, 29-30
buddy system, 31-32, 110-112
fostering classroom involvement,
    31-38
giving recognition, 30-31
involving others, 109-122
involving parents, 19-20, 29-30,
    117-119
labeling items, 28
learning and, 124-125
native language speakers, 29-30
parental involvement in class,
    19-20, 29-30
relaxation in, 86-87
risk taking, 27-28
setting routines, 31
small-group setting, 32-34, 62
speaking in front of the class,
    33-34
structured responses, 34
teacher's relationship with stu-
    dents, 6-9
using multicultural materials, 29
See also Teaching strategies
Closed questions, 7-8
Code-switching, 53-54
Cognates, 52
Cognitive Academic Language
    Learning Approach (CALLA),
    88-90
Cognitive academic language profi-
    ciency (CALP), 45
Collaborative learning style, 67
Collier, V., 80, 92, 135
Communication by students:
    in small-group setting, 32-33, 34
    speaking in front of the class,
        33-34
    See also Language development;
        Second-language develop-
        ment
Communication by teachers:
    appropriate level of, 43
    communication skills, 7-9

**CORWIN
PRESS**

The Corwin Press logo—a raven striding across an open book—represents the happy union of courage and learning. We are a professional-level publisher of books and journals for K-12 educators, and we are committed to creating and providing resources that embody these qualities. Corwin's motto is "Success for All Learners."